MW00477285

JAPANESE PHRASEBOOK & DICTIONARY

Published by Collins
An imprint of HarperCollins Publishers
Westerhill Road
Bishopbriggs
Glasgow G64 2QT

Third Edition 2017

10 9 8 7 6 5 4 3 2

© HarperCollins Publishers 2007, 2010, 2017

ISBN 978-0-00-813592-8

Collins® and Collins Gem® are registered trademarks of HarperCollins Publishers Limited

www.collinsdictionary.com

Typeset by Davidson Publishing Solutions, Glasgow

Printed and bound in China by RR Donnelley APS

All rights reserved. No part of this book may be reproduced, stored in a retrieval system, or transmitted in any form or by any means, electronic, mechanical, photocopying, recording or otherwise, without the prior permission in writing of the Publisher. This book is sold subject to the conditions that it shall not, by way of trade or otherwise, be lent, re-sold, hired out or otherwise circulated without the Publisher's prior consent in any form of binding or cover other than that in which it is published and without a similar condition including this condition being imposed on the subsequent purchaser.

Entered words that we have reason to believe constitute trademarks have been designated as such. However, neither the presence nor absence of such designation should be regarded as affecting the legal status of any trademark.

The contents of this publication are believed correct at the time of printing. Nevertheless, the Publisher can accept no responsibility for errors or omissions, changes in the detail given or for any expense or loss thereby caused.

HarperCollins does not warrant that any website mentioned in this title will be provided uninterrupted, that any website will be error free, that defects will be corrected, or that the website or the server that makes it available are free of viruses or bugs. For full terms and conditions please refer to the site terms provided on the website.

A catalogue record for this book is available from the British Library.

If you would like to comment on any aspect of this book, please contact us at the given address or online.

E-mail: dictionaries@harpercollins.co.uk
facebook.com/collinsdictionary
@collinsdict

Acknowledgements
We would like to thank those authors and publishers who kindly gave permission for copyright material to be used in the Collins Corpus. We would also like to thank Times Newspapers Ltd for providing valuable data.

Editor
Holly Tarbet

Contributors
Tessa Carroll
Harumi Currie
Miyoko Yamashita

For the Publisher
Gerry Breslin
Janice McNeillie

Front cover image:
Matsumoto Castle, Japan.
© Neale Cousland / Shutterstock.com.

Using your phrasebook

Whether you're on holiday or on business, your **Collins Gem Phrasebook and Dictionary** is designed to help you locate the exact phrase you need, when you need it. You'll also gain the confidence to go beyond what is in the book, as you can adapt the phrases by using the dictionary section to substitute your own words.

The **Gem Phrasebook and Dictionary** includes:

- Over 60 topics arranged thematically, so that you can easily find an expression to suit the situation
- Simple pronunciation which accompanies each word and phrase, to make sure you are understood when speaking aloud
- Tips to safeguard against any cultural faux pas, providing the essential dos and don'ts of local customs or etiquette
- A basic grammar section which will help you to build on your phrases
- **FACE TO FACE** dialogue sections to give you a flavour of what to expect from a real conversation
- **YOU MAY HEAR** sections for common announcements and messages, so that you don't miss important information when out and about

- A dictionary with over 1,000 words and their translations, to ensure you'll never be stuck for something to say
- **LIFELINE** phrases listed on the inside covers for quick reference. These basic words and phrases will be essential to your time abroad

Before you jet off, it's worth spending time looking through the topics to see what is covered and becoming familiar with pronunciation.

The colour key below shows you how to search the phrasebook by theme, so you'll be able to find relevant phrases very quickly.

Talking to people
Getting around
Staying somewhere
Shopping
Leisure
Communications
Practicalities
Health
Eating out
Menu reader
Reference
Grammar
Dictionary

Contents

Pronouncing Japanese

Although the Japanese writing system is rather complicated, pronouncing Japanese is easy once you know the few basic rules. This book has been designed so that as you read the pronunciation of the phrases, you can follow the Japanese. This will help you to recognize the different sounds and give you a feeling for the rhythm of the language. Below are a few rules for you to note.

In Japanese the basic unit of speech is the syllable. Each syllable is pronounced approximately the same length and rather flatly. Japanese has a pitched accent (high and low) but syllables do not have tones as they do in Chinese. It is more important not to stress any one part of a word. For example, in English the word Paris is pronounced **pa**ris and in French pa**ree**. Japanese gives equal strength to both syllables: **pa**r**i**.

Japanese has relatively few sounds. Each vowel has only one sound.

Japanese vowels

Japanese	sounds like	example
a	a	bath
i	i	police
u	u	put
e	e	let
o	o	got

Long vowel sounds

aa, ii, uu, ee, oo approximately double the length of other syllables

15 basic consonants

k, s, sh, t, ts, ch, n, h, m, y, r, w, g, z, d, b, p, n/m
Each consonant is followed by one vowel to create a syllable as in
ki-mo-no traditional Japanese costume
Ta-na-ka Japanese surname

These consonants are close to their English equivalents but note the following:
g is pronounced as in **g**olf, not as in **G**ermany
y is pronounced as in **y**oung, not as in cr**y**.

The consonant n/m, which appears at the end of the list above, counts as a syllable in its own right. It is pronounced like the nasal n in si**n**g when it appears at the end of words, e.g. e**n** 'yen', and before most other sounds, e.g. o**n**se**n** 'hot spring'. Before p, b and m, it sounds more like m and is therefore written here as m, e.g. shi**m**bun 'newspaper'. When n appears before a vowel or y, it is written as n' to distinguish it from the syllables beginning with n, e.g. ki**n'**en 'non-smoking' compared with ki**n**en 'commemoration'.

Since Japanese lacks the consonants **l** and **v**, foreign loanwords with these letters are pronounced with **r** and **b**, respectively. Thus, English words 'love' and 'rub' both become indistinguishable as ra-bu in Japanese.

Japanese also lacks the **si** sound (as in 'to sit'): shi is used instead, sometimes with embarrassing results! Other English sounds that do not exist in Japanese are **hu** (as in 'hook': fu is used instead); **th** (as in 'thin': shi is used instead); and **ti** (as in 'tin': chi is used instead).

Double consonants kk, pp, ss and tt are written before a vowel, which indicates a pause equivalent to one syllable in length before that consonant. The sound before the pause tends to become sharper than at other times.

Japanese	Pronunciation	Meaning
kitte	ki (pause) te	stamp
kippu	ki (pause) pu	ticket

ki, **shi**, **chi**, **ni**, **hi**, **mi**, **ri**, **gi**, **ji**, **bi** and **pi** sounds can be combined with **ya**, **yu** or **yo** to create combined syllables. For example, **ki + ya** become **kya**, **ki + yu** become **kyu** and **ki + yo** become **kyo**. Examples of this can be found in the words **Tookyoo** and **Kyooto**, where the combined syllable is pronounced as two sounds, but said very quickly with the same length as one syllable.

Japanese	Pronunciation	Meaning
matchi	ma (pause) chi	match

In the case of the **chi** syllable, a double consonant sound is written as **tchi** as in the example above.

You should also remember that Japanese does not have a silent **e** at the end of a word such as in the English 'to take'. If 'take' is read as the Japanese word **take** (bamboo), it should be pronounced tah-keh. Similarly **sake** (rice wine), is pronounced sah-keh, etc.

However, the vowel **u** at the end of a word such as **desu** will sound very weak.

Top ten tips

1. Always remember to remove your shoes before entering someone's home. Before stepping on **tatami** matting, slippers must also be removed. Slippers must be changed when going to the toilet. Remember not to leave the toilet still wearing the toilet slippers, as it would be very embarrassing!

2. Always make sure that you do not have any holes in your socks or tights, as you may have to take your shoes off unexpectedly.

3. Shaking hands is uncommon in Japan; Japanese people greet each other by bowing. However, foreigners are sometimes greeted with a handshake.

4. **Sumimasen** is a word with many purposes: it can be used to attract someone's attention before making a request, or to get past people on a crowded train. It can also be used to say 'sorry'.

5. Credit cards are only accepted in the more expensive hotels, shops and restaurants.

6 If you receive a gift from a Japanese visitor, ask if you can open it before doing so. If you are invited to a Japanese person's house, make sure you take a gift-wrapped present with you.

7 You can only buy cigarettes and alcohol if you are over 20 years of age. You will be asked to produce ID to prove your age.

8 Japanese people tend not to use assertive words such as 'yes' and 'no'. Good alternatives are **ii desu ne**, which literally means 'that sounds good',for 'yes' and **chotto** for 'no'.

9 Cleanliness is important to Japanese people. Never drop or leave rubbish.

10 It's advisable that you carry proof of identity at all times, so make sure that you always have your passport with you.

Talking to people

Hello/goodbye, yes/no

In Japanese there is no exact equivalent for the word 'hello' – different greeting words are used based on the time of the day. Similarly, the word **chotto** (whose literal meaning is 'a bit') is influenced by body language: if said with one's head slightly tilted, it means 'no'.

Hello	こんにちは konnichiwa
Good morning	おはようございます ohayoo gozaimasu
Good evening	こんばんは kombanwa
Good night	おやすみなさい oyasuminasai
Goodbye	さようなら sayoonara
See you later	じゃまた ja mata

See you tomorrow	また明日 mata ashita
How are you?	お元気ですか ogenki desu ka?
Fine, thanks	はい、元気です hai, genki desu
And you, Mr/Ms...?	...さんは ...san wa?
Please	お願いします onegai shimasu
Thank you	ありがとう (ございます) arigatoo (gozaimasu)
You're welcome	どういたしまして doo itashimashite
Excuse me!	ごめんなさい gomennasai!
Sorry!	すみません sumimasen!
Yes	はい hai
No	いいえ iie
Um...	ちょっと… chotto...
Yes, please	はい、お願いします hai, onegai shimasu

No, thanks	いいえ、結構です iie, kekkoo desu
Sir...	…氏 ...shi
Mr.../Madam.../ Mrs.../Ms.../ Miss...	…さん ...san
I don't understand	わかりません wakarimasen
I don't speak Japanese	私は日本語を話せません watashi wa nihongo o hanasemasen
England/English	イングランド／イングランド人 ingurando/ingurando-jin
Scotland/Scottish	スコットランド／スコットランド人 sukottorando/sukottorando-jin
Wales/Welsh	ウェールズ／ウェールズ人 weeruzu/weeruzu-jin
Ireland/Irish	アイルランド／アイルランド人 airurando/airurando-jin
USA/American	アメリカ／アメリカ人 amerika/amerika-jin
Australia/ Australian	オーストラリア／オーストラリア人 oosutoraria/oosutoraria-jin

Bowing おじぎ ojigi

Japanese people bow to express their respect and appreciation. People bow along with greetings, words of appreciation or apologies. The strength of the respect, gratitude or apology, dictates how low your bow should be.

Key phrases

There are no genders, articles or singular/plural forms in Japanese. Different counters are used together with numbers.

museum	美術館 bijutsukan
the station	駅 eki
the shops	店 mise
the houses	家 ie/uchi
a/one	一つ hitotsu
a ticket	チケット一枚 chiketto ichimai

one stamp	切手一枚 kitte ichimai
a room	一部屋 hito heya
one bottle	一本 ippon
some (countable)	いくつか ikutsuka
some (uncountable)	いくらか ikuraka
some wine	ワインいくらか wain ikuraka
some fruit	フルーツいくつか furuutsu ikutsuka
some biscuits	ビスケットいくつか bisuketto ikutsuka
Do you have...?	…はありますか ...wa arimasu ka?
Do you have a timetable?	時刻表はありますか jikokuhyoo wa arimasu ka?
Do you have a room?	部屋はありますか heya wa arimasu ka?
Do you have milk?	牛乳はありますか gyuunyuu wa arimasu ka?
I/We'd like to...	…(動詞) たいです ...(*verb*) tai desu

I/We'd like...	…(名詞) をお願いします ...(*noun*) o onegai shimasu
I'd like an ice cream	アイスクリームをお願いします aisukuriimu o onegai shimasu
We'd like to go home	家に帰りたいです ie ni kaeritai desu
Another...	…おかわり ...okawari
Some more...	…もう少し ...moo sukoshi
Some more bread	パン、もう少し pan moo sukoshi
Another Japanese tea	お茶、おかわり ocha okawari
Another beer	ビール、おかわり biiru okawari
Some more water	お水、もう少し omizu moo sukoshi
How much is it?	これはいくらですか kore wa ikura desu ka?
large	大きい ookii
small	小さい chiisai
with	と to

without	抜きで nukide
Where is/are...?	…はどこですか ... wa doko desu ka?
Where is/are the nearest...?	一番近い … はどこですか ichiban chikai ... wa doko desu ka?
How do I get to...?	…へはどうやって行きますか ...ewa dooyatte ikimasu ka?
to the museum	美術館へは bijutsukan ewa
to the station	駅へは eki ewa
to Kyoto	京都へは Kyooto ewa
There is/are...	…があります ...ga arimasu
There isn't/ aren't any...	…がありません ...ga arimasen
When?	いつ itsu?
At what time...?	何時に… nan-ji ni...?
today	今日 kyoo
tomorrow	明日 ashita

May I...?	…もいいですか ...mo ii desu ka?
May I smoke?	タバコを吸ってもいいですか tabako o sutte mo ii desu ka?
How does this work?	これはどうやって使いますか kore wa dooyatte tsukaimasu ka?
What does this mean?	これはどういう意味ですか kore wa doo iu imi desu ka?

Work

Japanese people tend to tell you where they work rather than what they do.

Where do you work?	お勤めはどちらですか otsutome wa dochira desu ka?
How's your work?	仕事はどうですか shigoto wa doo desu ka?
I'm...	私は… watashi wa...
a doctor	医者です isha desu
a manager	マネージャーです maneejaa desu
a housewife	主婦です shufu desu

I work from home	私は在宅勤務です watashi wa zaitaku-kimmu desu
I'm self-employed	私は自営業です watashi wa jieigyoo desu

Weather

天気予報 tenki-yohoo	weather forecast
晴れ hare	fine
悪い warui	bad
曇り kumori	cloudy
変わりやすい天気 kawariyasui tenki	changeable weather

sunny	天気がいいです tenki ga ii desu
It's muggy	蒸し暑いです mushiatsui desu
It's raining	雨が降っています ame ga futte imasu
It's snowing	雪が降っています yuki ga futte imasu
It's windy	風が強いです kaze ga tsuyoi desu

What a lovely day!	なんていい日 nante ii hi!
What awful weather!	なんてひどい天気 nante hidoi tenki!
What will the weather be like tomorrow?	明日の天気はどうですか ashita no tenki wa doo desu ka?
Do you think it's going to rain?	雨が降りそうですか ame ga furisoo desu ka?
It's very hot today	今日はとても暑いです kyoo wa totemo atsui desu
It's very cold today	今日はとても寒いです kyoo wa totemo samui desu
Do you think there will be a storm?	嵐になると思いますか arashi ni naru to omoimasu ka?
Do you think it will snow?	雪になると思いますか yuki ni naru to omoimasu ka?
Will it be foggy?	霧になると思いますか kiri ni naru to omoimasu ka?
What is the temperature?	気温は何度ですか kion wa nando desu ka?

Getting around

Asking the way

反対 hantai	opposite
…の隣 ...no tonari	next to...
…の近く ...no chikaku	near to...
信号 shingoo	traffic lights
横断歩道 oodan-hodoo	pedestrian crossing
(道路の) 角 (dooro no) kado	corner (of road)

FACE TO FACE

すみません、駅までどうやって行きますか
sumimasen, eki made dooyatte ikimasu ka?
Excuse me, how do I get to the station?

まっすぐ行って、一つ目の角を右/
左に曲がってください
massugu itte, hitotsu-me no kado o migi/
hidari ni magatte kudasai
Keep straight on, turn right/left at the first corner

遠いですか
tooi desu ka?
Is it far?

いいえ、200メートル/5分くらいです
iie, nihyaku-meetoru/go-fun kurai desu
No, about 200 metres/five minutes

ありがとう
arigatoo!
Thank you!

どういたしまして
doo itashimashite
You're welcome

We're lost	道に迷ってしまいました michi ni mayotte shimaimashita
We're looking for...	…を探しています ...o sagashite imasu
Is this the right way to...?	…に行くのはこれでいいですか ...ni iku no wa kore de ii desu ka?
Can I/we walk there?	そこまで歩けますか soko made arukemasu ka?
How do I/ we get...?	どうすれば … に行けますか doo sureba ... ni ikemasu ka?
to the station	駅に eki ni
to the museum	美術館に bijutsukan ni

to the shops	お店に omise ni
Can you show me on the map?	地図で示してもらえますか chizu de shimeshite moraemasu ka?

YOU MAY HEAR...	
下った所 kudatta tokoro	down there
後ろ ushiro	behind
もう一度聞いてください moo ichido kiite kudasai	then ask again

Bus and coach

Places such as Kyoto have tourist day passes and bus route maps in English, which you can obtain at a bus station. Local buses usually board from the rear door, but if your journey is not covered by a flat fee you may need to pick up a numbered ticket. A board at the front of the bus displays the fares, based on the numbers. You will need to know your destination in Japanese characters. Some buses board from the front door and require you to pay as you enter. Tickets for long/middle distance coach trips, as well as express buses, are usually sold at the coach counter or ticketing machine.

FACE TO FACE

すみません、どのバスが中心部に行きますか
sumimasen, dono basu ga chuushimbu ni ikimasu ka?
Excuse me, which bus goes to the centre?

15番です
juugo-ban desu
Number 15

バス停はどこですか
basutei wa doko desu ka?
Where is the bus stop?

すぐそこ、右にあります
sugu soko, migi ni arimasu
There, on the right

どこで乗車券を買えますか
doko de jooshaken o kaemasu ka?
Where can I buy the tickets?

売店で買えます
baiten de kaemasu
At the news-stand

Is there a bus/ tram to...?	…に行くバス/ 路面電車はありますか ...ni iku basu/romen-densha wa arimasu ka?

Where do I/ we catch the bus to...?	どこで … 行きのバスに乗れますか doko de ... iki no basu ni noremasu ka?
Where do I/ we catch the tram to...?	どこで … 行きの路面電車に乗れますか doko de ... iki no romen-densha ni noremasu ka?
I/we would like to go to...	…に行きたいんですが ...ni ikitain desu ga
How much is it to go to...?	…までいくらですか ...made ikura desu ka?
the centre	中心部 chuushimbu
the beach	浜辺 hamabe
How often are the buses to...?	…に行くバスはどのぐらい出ていますか ...ni iku basu wa donogurai dete imasu ka?
When is the first bus to...?	…行きの始発バスはいつですか ...iki no shihatsu basu wa itsu desu ka?
When is the last bus to...?	…行きの最終バスはいつですか ...iki no saishuu basu wa itsu desu ka?

Please tell me when to get off	いつ降りたらいいか教えてください itsu oritara ii ka oshiete kudasai
Please tell me when we are at...	…に着いたら教えてください ...ni tsuitara oshiete kudasai
Please let me off	すみません、降ろしてください sumimasen, oroshite kudasai
I got on at...	…から乗りました ...kara norimashita
Sorry, I forgot to take a ticket (on entering bus)	すみません、整理券を取りませんでした sumimasen, seiriken o torimasen deshita
coach	長距離バス chookyori-basu
shuttle bus	シャトルバス shatoru-basu

YOU MAY HEAR...

ここ/このバス停ですよ koko/kono basutei desu yo	This is it/your stop
地下鉄の方が、速いですよ chikatetsu no hoo ga hayai desu yo	Take the metro, it's quicker

Public transport is free for up to two children under 6 when travelling with a paying adult. An elementary school pupil pays half price (aged between 7 and 12). Junior high (13 to 15) and senior high (16 to 18) school students are often given discounts too.

Metro

The Japanese metro and train services are clean, safe and run on time. You can find metro systems in the Tokyo area, as well as Sapporo, Yokohama, Nagoya, Kyoto, Osaka, and several other cities. You can either purchase a pre-paid card or an ordinary ticket from the ticketing machine. Silver seats are for elderly people or people with difficulties. Mobile phones need to be on silent and you must not talk in the carriage. In major cities, the rush hour crush can be really bad (between 7 and 9 am and 5 and 8 pm). Some trains have women-only carriages. The Japanese metro system is very similar to the one in London. **Suika** is like the Oyster card. The first thing you must do is obtain a metro map which indicates all the lines and stops.

入口	iriguchi	entrance
出口	deguchi	way out/exit

Can I get a seat reservation please?	座席の予約をお願いします zaseki no yoyaku o onegai shimasu?
Where can I get a ticket?	切符はどこで買えますか kippu wa doko de kaemasu ka?
Where is the nearest metro station?	一番近い地下鉄の駅はどこですか ichiban chikai chikatetsu no eki wa doko desu ka?
How does the ticket machine work?	券売機はどうやって使いますか kembaiki wa dooyatte tsukaimasu ka?
I'm going to...	…に行きます ...ni ikimasu
Do you have a map of the metro?	地下鉄の地図はありますか chikatetsu no chizu wa arimasu ka?
How do I get to...?	どうやって … に行きますか dooyatte ... ni ikimasu ka?
Do I have to change?	乗り換えはありますか norikae wa arimasu ka?
Does this go to...?	これは … に行きますか kore wa ... ni ikimasu ka?
Which line is it for...?	…行きは何線ですか ...iki wa nan-sen desu ka?

Which platform is it for...?	…行きは何番線ですか ...iki wa nan-bansen desu ka?
What is the next stop?	次の駅はどこですか tsugi no eki wa doko desu ka?
Excuse me!	すみません sumimasen!
Please let me out	降ろしてください oroshite kudasai

Train

You will find **Midori no madoguchi** (literally 'Green Ticket Window') in major train stations, where you can buy tickets and make seat bookings. You need to pay a supplement in order to use an express train. There are seven lines of **Shinkansen**, high-speed (bullet) train, and they serve areas from Hokkaido to Kyushu. It is expensive to travel around Japan using the **Shinkansen**, so a JR Pass could save you money. With this pass, you can cover a considerable distance around Japan. Details can be found at **www.japanrailpass.net**.

各駅停車	kakueki teisha	slow stopping train (stops at all stations)

快速/特別快速電車 kaisoku/tokubetsu kaisoku densha	**local train** (stops at selected stations)
準急/急行電車 junkyuu/kyuukoo densha	**semi-express/express** (stops at main stations: supplement)
特急電車 tokkyuu densha	**intercity** (stops at main intercity stations: supplement)
新幹線 shinkansen	**high-speed bullet train**
ホーム hoomu	**platform**
窓口 madoguchi	**ticket office**
時刻表 jikokuhyoo	**timetable**
遅れ okure	**delay** (appears on train noticeboards)
手荷物一時預かり tenimotsu ichiji azukari	**left luggage**
eチケット ii-chiketto	**e-ticket**
オンライン予約 onrain-yoyaku	**e-booking**

You can buy a Japan Rail Pass (JR Pass) Exchange Order in your own country, which needs to be exchanged for the Japan Rail Pass itself when you get to Japan. The stations where you can exchange the Order are shown on the back.

FACE TO FACE

次の … 行きの電車は何時ですか
tsugi no ... iki no densha wa nan-ji desu ka?
What time is the next train to...?

17時10分です
juushichi-ji juppun desu
At 17.10

切符を3枚ください
kippu o san-mai kudasai
I'd like 3 tickets, please

片道ですか、往復ですか
katamichi desu ka, oofuku desu ka?
Single or return?

Where is the station?	駅はどこですか eki wa doko desu ka?
to...	…行き ...iki
I booked online	オンラインで予約しました onrain de yoyaku shimashita
a single	片道一枚 katamichi ichi-mai
two returns	往復二枚 oofuku ni-mai
reserved seat	指定席 shitei-seki

non-reserved seat	自由席 jiyuu-seki
first class	グリーン 車 guriin-sha
standard class	普通車 futsuu-sha
smoking	喫煙 kitsuen
non-smoking	禁煙 kin'en
I want to book a seat on the bullet train to Tokyo	東京まで新幹線の指定席を予約したいんですが tookyoo made shinkansen no shitei-seki o yoyaku shitain desu ga
Do I have to change?	乗り換えがありますか norikae ga arimasu ka?
How long is there to wait for the connection?	乗り換え時間はどのくらいありますか norikae-jikan wa donokurai arimasu ka?
Is this the train for...?	これは … 行きの電車ですか kore wa ... iki no densha desu ka?
Why is the train delayed?	なぜ電車は遅れているのですか naze densha wa okurete iru no desu ka?

When will it leave?	いつ出発しますか itsu shuppatsu shimasu ka?
Does it stop at...?	…に停まりますか ...ni tomarimasu ka?
When does it arrive in...?	…にはいつ着きますか ...niwa itsu tsukimasu ka?
Please tell me when we get to...	…に着いたら教えてください ...ni tsuitara oshiete kudasai
Is there a restaurant car?	食堂車はありますか shokudoo-sha wa arimasu ka?
Is this seat free?	この席は空いていますか kono seki wa aite imasu ka?
Excuse me! (to get past)	すみません sumimasen!

Taxi

Japanese taxis are safe, clean and operate on meters. The basic fee is based on the vehicle size. For different sizes of taxi, you can ask for 小型 (kogata) for up to four passengers and 中型 (chuugata) for up to five. It can be rather expensive but there is no need to tip. There are taxi stands at stations and major hotels but taxis can also be hailed from the roadside. You can identify whether a taxi is available by the sign 空車 (kuusha) displayed in the front windscreen. All the doors are automatically operated by the driver. There are many regional taxi companies, and vehicles vary in colour depending on the company.

I want a taxi	タクシーに乗りたいです takushii ni noritai desu
Where can I get a taxi?	タクシー乗り場はどこですか takushii noriba wa doko desu ka?
Please order me a taxi	タクシーを呼んでください takushii o yonde kudasai
now	今 ima
for...(time)	…(時) に ...(ji) ni
How much will it cost to go to...?	…までいくらかかりますか ...made ikura kakarimasu ka?
How long will it take?	どのくらいかかりますか donokurai kakarimasu ka?
vacant (car)	空車 kuusha
to the station please	駅までお願いします eki made onegai shimasu
to the airport please	空港までお願いします kuukoo made onegai shimasu

to this address please	この住所までお願いします kono juusho made onegai shimasu
How much is it?	いくらですか ikura desu ka?
Can I have a receipt please?	レシートをお願いします reshiito o onegai shimasu?
Keep the change	おつりは結構です otsuri wa kekkoo desu
Sorry, I don't have any change	すみません、小銭がありません sumimasen, kozeni ga arimasen

Boat and ferry

Japan Railways (JR) run ferry services on certain routes where the JR Pass can be used. There is a good ferry network in Japan linking the various islands. Ferries can be used as an alternative to trains if you wish to travel between the islands and have time to spare. During the holidays some lines can be very busy, so if you are driving it is advisable to book a place in advance.

Do you have a timetable?	時刻表はありますか jikokuhyoo wa arimasu ka?
Is there a car ferry to...?	…に行くカーフェリーはありますか ...ni iku kaa-ferii wa arimasu ka?

How much is a ticket...?	切符はいくらですか kippu wa ikura desu ka?
single	片道 katamichi
return	往復 oofuku
How much is it for a car and ... people?	車と人が … 人でいくらですか kuruma to hito ga ... nin de ikura desu ka?
one person	一人 hitori
two people	二人 futari
three people	三人 san-nin
Where does the boat leave from?	ボートはどこから出ますか booto wa doko kara demasu ka?
Are there any boat trips around Tokyo bay?	東京湾の遊覧船はありますか tookyoo-wan no yuuransen wa arimasu ka?
When is the next boat?	次の船は何時ですか tsugi no fune wa nan-ji desu ka?
How long does the trip take?	遊覧はどのくらいかかります か yuuran wa donokurai kakarimasu ka?

YOU MAY HEAR...	
これが最終便です kore ga saishuu-bin desu	This is the last boat
今日はやっていません kyoo wa yatte imasen	There is no service today
車は何ですか kuruma wa nan desu ka?	What type of car do you have?

Air travel

At the airport, most signs are written in both Japanese and English. Most of the airport staff understand and speak some English. The three biggest airports are **Narita**, **Kansai** and **Haneda**. You can find airport details by visiting **www.narita-airport.jp**, **www.kansai-airport.jp** and **www.haneda-airport.jp**.

到着 toochaku	arrivals
出発 shuppatsu	departures
国際 kokusai	international
国内 kokunai	domestic
搭乗口 toojooguchi	boarding gate

How do I/we go to...?	…にはどうやって行けばいいですか ...niwa dooyatte ikeba ii desu ka?
to the airport	空港には kuukoo niwa
to town	街には machi niwa
to the hotel...	…ホテルには ...hoteru niwa
to the ... airport	…空港には ...kuukoo niwa
checked luggage	預かり荷物 azukarinimotsu
hand luggage	手荷物 tenimotsu
Is there a bus to the airport?	空港行きのバスはありますか kuukoo iki no basu wa arimasu ka?
Where is the check-in desk for...?	…のチックインカウンターはどこですか ...no chekku-in kauntaa wa doko desu ka?
Which carousel is for the luggage for the flight from...?	…から着いた荷物はどのターンテーブルですか ...kara tsuita nimotsu wa dono taanteeburu desu ka?

Where can I change some money?	お金の両替はどこでできますか okane no ryoogae wa doko de dekimasu ka?
Where can I print my ticket?	チケットの印刷はどこでできますか chiketto no insatsu wa doko de dekimasu ka?
I have my boarding pass on my smartphone	搭乗券はスマホに入っています toojooken wa sumaho ni haitte imasu

YOU MAY HEAR...	
…番ゲートから搭乗します ...ban geeto kara toojoo shimasu	Boarding will take place at gate number...
番ゲートまで至急お進みください ...ban geeto made shikyuu osusumi kudasai	Go immediately to gate number...
液体物禁止 ekitaibutsu-kinshi	No liquids
荷物が重量制限をオーバーしています nimotsu ga juuryoo seigen o oobaa shite imasu	Your luggage exceeds the maximum weight

Customs control

UK, US, Canadian and Australian visitors to Japan do not require a visa for short business trips and holidays. During your stay, you are not allowed to work. It is advisable that you have proof of identity at all times, so make sure that you always carry your passport.

日本人帰国 nihon-jin kikoku	Japanese people returning to the country
外国人入国 gaikoku-jin nyuukoku	Non-Japanese people entering the country
税関 zeikan	customs

Do I have to pay duty on this?	これに税金がかかりますか kore ni zeikin ga kakarimasu ka?
It's for my own personal use	私が使う物です watashi ga tsukau mono desu
It's a present	プレゼントです purezento desu
I have nothing to declare	申告する物はありません shinkoku suru mono wa arimasen
We are on our way to... (if in transit through a country)	…に行く途中です ...ni iku tochuu desu

My passport	私のパスポート watashi no pasupooto
My visa	私のビザ watashi no biza
I came here on...	…で来ました ...de kimashita
holiday	休暇 kyuuka
business	仕事 shigoto

Car hire

You must obtain an international driving permit prior to leaving your country. You also need to carry your own national licence while driving in Japan. You will be required to produce your international driving permit to rent a car.

運転免許証 unten-menkyoshoo	driving licence
総合保険 soogoohoken	fully comprehensive insurance

I want to hire a car	車をかりたいです kuruma o karitai desu

for ... days	…日 ...nichi
with automatic gears	オートマ車 ootoma sha
What are your rates...?	…料金はいくらですか ...ryookin wa ikura desu ka?
per day	一日の ichinichi no
per week	一週間の isshuukan no
How much is the deposit?	保証金はいくらですか hoshookin wa ikura desu ka?
Do you take credit cards?	クレジットカードは使えますか kurejitto kaado wa tsukaemasu ka?
Is there a charge per mile/ kilometre?	走行距離の支払いはありますか sookoo-kyori no shiharai wa arimasu ka?
Does the price include fully comprehensive insurance?	この金額は総合保険料を含んでいますか kono kingaku wa soogoohoken-ryoo o fukunde imasu ka?
Must I return the car here?	車はここに返さなければいけませんか kuruma wa koko ni kaesanakereba ikemasen ka?

By what time?	何時までにですか nan-ji made ni desu ka?
I'd like to leave it in...	… に置いてきたいです ... ni oite kitai desu

YOU MAY HEAR...	
車はガソリンを満タンにして返してください kuruma wa gasorin o mantan ni shite kaeshite kudasai	Please return the car with a full tank

Driving

Can I/we park here?	ここに駐車してもいいですか koko ni chuusha shite mo ii desu ka?
How long for?	どのくらいまで donokurai made?
Which junction is it for...?	…に行くにはどのジャンクションですか ...ni iku niwa dono jankushon desu ka?
Do I/we need snow chains?	チェーンは必要ですか cheen wa hitsuyoo desu ka?

Petrol

In Japan, the majority of petrol stations are manned by attendants who not only fill up the tank for you but also wipe the windows and check the water. However, unmanned petrol stations have been on the rise recently and are cheaper than manned ones.

ハイオク haioku	4 star
ディーゼル diizeru	diesel
無鉛 muen	unleaded

Fill it up, please	満タンにしてください mantan ni shite kudasai
Please check...	…をチェックしてください ...o chekku shite kudasai
the oil	オイル oiru
the water	水 mizu
3000 yen worth of unleaded petrol	3000円分の無鉛ガソリン sanzen en bun no muen gasorin
Where is...?	…はどこですか ...wa doko desu ka?

Can I pay by credit card?	クレジットカードで払えますか kurejitto kaado de haraemasu ka?

YOU MAY HEAR...	
オイル/水が必要です oiru/mizu ga hitsuyoo desu	You need some oil/ some water
全て大丈夫です subete daijoobu desu	Everything is OK

Breakdown

If you break down, the emergency telephone number for the Japanese equivalent of the AA (JAF – Japan Automobile Federation) is **0570-00-8139** or # (hash key) **8139**

Can you help me?	助けてもらえますか tasukete moraemasu ka?
My car has broken down	車が故障してしまいました kuruma ga koshoo shite shimaimashita
I've run out of petrol	ガソリンがきれてしまいました gasorin ga kirete shimaimashita

Can you tow me to the nearest garage?	最寄のガソリンスタンドまで引っぱって行ってもらえますか moyori no gasorin-sutando made hippatte itte moraemasu ka?
Do you have parts for a (make of car)...?	…の部品がありますか ...no buhin ga arimasu ka?
There's something wrong with the...	…に何かおかしいところがあります ...ni nanika okashii tokoro ga arimasu
Can you replace...?	…を交換できますか ...o kookan dekimasu ka?

Car parts

The ... isn't/aren't working properly	…の調子が悪いです ...no chooshi ga warui desu

accelerator	アクセル	akuseru
alternator	オルタネーター	orutaneetaa
battery	バッテリー	batterii
bonnet	ボンネット	bonnetto
brakes	ブレーキ	bureeki
choke	チョーク	chooku
clutch	クラッチ	kurattchi

distributor	配電器	haidenki
engine	エンジン	enjin
exhaust	エキゾースト	ekizoosuto
fuse	ヒューズ	hyuuzu
gears	ギア	gia
handbrake	ハンドブレーキ	hando bureeki
headlights	ヘッドライト	heddo raito
ignition	点火装置	tenka soochi
indicator	方向指示器	hookoo shijiki
points	ポイント	pointo
radiator	ラジエーター	rajieetaa
reverse gear	バックギア	bakku gia
seat belt	シートベルト	shiito beruto
spark plug	点火プラグ	tenka puragu
steering	ステアリング	sutearingu
steering wheel	ハンドル	handoru
tyre	タイヤ	taiya
wheel	車輪	sharin
windscreen	フロントガラス	furonto garasu
windscreen washer	ウインドウウォッシャー	uindoo wosshaa
windscreen wiper	ワイパー	waipaa

Road signs

no thoroughfare

closed to pedestrians

stopping permitted

centre line

drive slowly

stop

bicycle crossing

minimum speed

pedestrian crossing

two-step right turn for motorcycles

stop line

safety zone

Staying somewhere

Hotel (booking)

Japan offers a wide choice of places to stay, from western-style hotels to traditional Japanese inns. Capsule hotels offer minimum sleeping space on multiple levels, but have all the facilities and are good value for money.

YOU MAY HEAR...	
シングルルーム shinguru ruumu	single room
ダブルルーム daburu ruumu	double room
洋室 yooshitsu	western-style room
和室 washitsu	Japanese-style room
大人の人数 otona no ninzuu	number of adults
子供の人数 kodomo no ninzuu	number of children

カプセルホテル kapuseru hoteru	capsule hotel
旅館　ryokan	traditional Japanese inn
宿坊　shukuboo	a stay in a shrine/ temple
ユースホステル yuusuhosuteru	youth hostel

How much is it per night/ per week?	一泊/一週間いくらですか ippaku/isshuukan ikura desu ka?
Do you have a room for tonight?	今夜泊まれますか kon'ya tomaremasu ka?
with bath	お風呂付き ofuro tsuki
with shower	シャワー付き shawaa tsuki
with a double bed	ダブルベッド付き daburu beddo tsuki
with twin beds and an extra bed for a child	ツインベッドと子供用のエクストラベッド tsuin beddo to kodomo-yoo no ekusutra beddo
Is breakfast included?	朝ごはんは含まれていますか asa-gohan wa fukumarete imasu ka?

Have you got anything cheaper?	もう少し安いのはありますか moo sukoshi yasui no wa arimasu ka?

FACE TO FACE

シングル/ダブルルームを予約したいんですが
shinguru/daburu ruumu o yoyaku shitain desu ga
I'd like to book a single/double room

何泊ですか
nampaku desu ka?
For how many nights?

一泊です/…泊です/…から…までです
ippaku desu/...haku (paku) desu/...kara...made desu
For one night/...nights/from...till...

YOU MAY HEAR...

満室です manshitsu desu shimasu	We're full
お名前をお願いします onamae o onegai shimasu	Your name, please
…の確認をお願いします ...no kakunin o onegai	Please confirm...
メールで meeru de	by e-mail
電話で denwa de	by phone

Hotel desk

The Japan National Tourist Organization and Tourist Information Centre can help with finding accommodation. Visit www.jnto.go.jp.

I booked a room...	…の部屋を予約しました ...no heya o yoyaku shimashita
in the name of...	…の名前で ...no namae de
Where can I park the car?	どこに車を停められますか doko ni kuruma o tomeraremasu ka?
What time is...?	…は何時ですか ...wa nan-ji desu ka?
dinner	夕食 yuushoku
breakfast	朝食 chooshoku
The key please	鍵をお願いします kagi o onegai shimasu
Room number...	部屋番号は… heya bangoo wa...
I'm leaving tomorrow	明日発ちます ashita tachimasu

I reserved the room(s) online	部屋をインターネットで予約しました heya o intaanetto de yoyaku shimashita
Does the price include breakfast?	朝食込みの料金ですか chooshoku-komi no ryookin desu ka?
Is there a hotel restaurant/bar?	ホテルにレストラン／バーがありますか hoteru ni resutoran/baa ga arimasu ka?

Camping

ごみ gomi	rubbish
飲料水 inryoosui	drinking water
コンセント konsento	electric point

Is there ... on the campsite?	キャンプ場に … はありますか kyampujoo ni ... wa arimasu ka?
a restaurant	レストラン resutoran
a self-service café	セルフサービスの食堂 serufu-saabisu no shokudoo

Do you have any vacancies?	空きはありますか aki wa arimasu ka?
How much is it...?	…いくらですか ...ikura desu ka?
per night	一泊 ippaku
per tent	テントあたり tento atari
per caravan	キャラバンあたり kyaraban atari
per person	一人あたり hitori atari
Does the price include...?	…の料金は含まれていますか ...no ryookin wa fukumarete imasu ka?
showers	シャワー shawaa
hot water	お湯 oyu
electricity	電気 denki

Self-catering

There are short-stay apartments in Japan called 'weekly mansions' and 'monthly mansions'. These are somewhat upmarket, boutique stays. There are inexpensive self-catering accommodation options such as guest houses (**gaijin**). You'll be able to find more information on **www.japan-guide.com**.

Who do we contact if there are problems?	何か問題があった場合、誰に連絡すればいいですか nani ka mondai ga atta baai, dare ni renraku sureba ii desu ka?
How does the heating work?	ヒーターはどうやって使いますか hiitaa wa dooyatte tsukaimasu ka?
Is there always hot water?	お湯はいつでもでますか oyu wa itsudemo demasu ka?
Where is the nearest supermarket?	最寄のスーパーはどこですか moyori no suupaa wa doko desu ka?
Where do we leave the rubbish?	ごみはどこに捨てればいいですか gomi wa doko ni sutereba ii desu ka?
recycling	リサイクル risaikuru

Shopping

Shopping phrases

Most department stores open from 10 am to 8 pm or later. The longer opening hours are often at the weekends, in summer and at the end of the year. Some shops are open 24 hours, including the **kombini** convenience stores.

FACE TO FACE

何をお求めですか
nani o omotome desu ka?
What would you like?

…はありますか
...wa arimasu ka?
Do you have...?

はい、こちらになります。他に何か
hai, kochira ni narimasu. hoka ni nani ka?
Certainly, here you are. Anything else?

Where is...?	…はどこですか ...wa doko desu ka?

I'm just looking	見ているだけです mite iru dake desu
Where can I buy...?	…はどこで買えますか ...wa doko de kaemasu ka?
shoes	靴 kutsu
gifts	ギフト gifuto
Do you have anything...?	もう少し … ものはありますか moo sukoshi ... mono wa arimasu ka?
larger	大きい ookii
smaller	小さい chiisai

Shops

セール seeru	sale
割引 waribiki	discount
祝日休業 shukujitsu kyuugyoo	closed for holidays

baker's	パン屋	pan-ya
bookshop	本屋	hon-ya
butcher's	肉屋	niku-ya

cake shop	ケーキ屋	keeki-ya
clothes shop	洋服屋	yoofuku-ya
department store	デパート	depaato
fruit shop	果物屋	kudamono-ya
gift shop	ギフトショップ	gifuto-shoppu
grocer's	食料品店	shokuryoo hinten
hairdresser's	美容院	biyooin
hypermarket	大型スーパーマーケット	oogata-suupaa-maaketto
newsagent	新聞販売所	shimbun hambai-jo
optician	メガネ屋	megane-ya
cosmetics shop	化粧品屋	keshoohin-ya
pharmacy	薬局	yakkyoku
photographic shop	写真屋	shashin-ya
shoe shop	靴屋	kutsu-ya
souvenir shop	土産物屋	miyagemono-ya
sports shop	スポーツショップ	supootsu shoppu
supermarket	スーパー	suupaa
tobacconist's	タバコ屋	tabako-ya
toy shop	おもちゃ屋	omocha-ya

Food (general)

biscuits	ビスケット	bisuketto
bread	パン	pan
bread (for toast)	食パン	shoku pan
sweet bread	菓子パン	kashi pan
butter	バター	bataa
cheese	チーズ	chiizu
chicken	チキン	chikin
coffee	コーヒー	koohii
cream	クリーム	kuriimu
crisps	ポテトチップス	poteto-chippusu
eggs	たまご	tamago
fish	魚	sakana
ham	ハム	hamu
ham (uncured)	生ハム	nama-hamu
herbal tea	ハーブティー	haabu tii
jam	ジャム	jamu
margarine	マーガリン	maagarin
marmalade	マーマレード	maamareedo
milk	ミルク	miruku
oil	油	abura
orange juice	オレンジジュース	orenji juusu

pepper	こしょう	koshoo
salt	しお	shio
sugar	さとう	satoo
Japanese tea	お茶	ocha
English tea	紅茶	koocha
vinegar	酢	su
yoghurt	ヨーグルト	yooguruto

Food (fruit and veg)

Fruit

apples	りんご	ringo
apricots	アプリコット	apurikotto
bananas	バナナ	banana
cherries	さくらんぼ	sakurambo
grapefruit	グレープフルーツ	gureepufuruutsu
grapes	ぶどう	budoo
lemon	レモン	remon
melon	メロン	meron
oranges	オレンジ	orenji
peaches	桃	momo
pears	梨	nashi
plums	すもも	sumomo

raspberries	ラズベリー	razuberii
strawberries	いちご	ichigo
watermelon	すいか	suika

Vegetables

asparagus	アスパラガス	asuparagasu
aubergine	なす	nasu
carrots	にんじん	ninjin
cauliflower	カリフラワー	karifurawaa
celery	セロリ	serori
courgettes	ズッキーニ	zukkiini
cucumber	きゅうり	kyuuri
garlic	にんにく	ninniku
mushrooms	きのこ	kinoko
onions	たまねぎ	tamanegi
peas	エンドウ	endoo
pepper	ピーマン	piiman
potatoes	じゃがいも	jagaimo
runner beans	インゲン	ingen
salad	サラダ	sarada
spinach	ほうれん草	hoorensoo
spring onions	ねぎ	negi
tomatoes	トマト	tomato

Clothes

The table below is a guideline only; in Japan the size can vary by style or brand.

women's sizes		men's sizes		shoe sizes			
UK	Japan	UK	Japan	UK	Japan	UK	Japan
8	7	34	S	2	22	7	25.5
10	9	36	M	3	22.5	8	26.5
12	11	38	L	4	23	9	27.5
14	13	40	LL/XL	5	24	10	28
16	15			6	24.5	11	28.5
18	17						

FACE TO FACE

試着してみてもいいですか
shichaku shite mite mo ii desu ka?
May I try this on?

どうぞ、こちらに
doozo, kochira ni
Please come this way

S/M/Lサイズはありますか
esu/emu/eru saizu wa arimasu ka?
Do you have a small/medium/large size?

サイズは何ですか
saizu wan nan desu ka?
What size (clothes) do you take?

bigger	もっと大きい motto ookii
smaller	もっと小さい motto chiisai
in other colours	他の色で hoka no iro de

YOU MAY HEAR...	
靴のサイズはいくつですか kutsu no saizu wa ikutsu desu ka?	What shoe size do you take?
この色はこのサイズしかありません kono iro wa kono saizu shika arimasen	In this colour we only have this size

Clothes (articles)

blouse	ブラウス	burausu
coat	コート	kooto
dress	ワンピース	wanpiisu
jacket	ジャケット	jaketto
jumper	セーター	seetaa
knickers	パンティー	pantii

shirt	シャツ	shatsu
shorts	半ズボン	hanzubon
skirt	スカート	sukaato
socks	ソックス	sokkusu
swimsuit	水着	mizugi
t-shirt	Tシャツ	tii shatsu
trousers	ズボン	zubon

Maps and guides

キオスク kiosuku	kiosk
週刊誌 shuukanshi	weekly magazine
新聞 shimbun	newspaper

Do you have a map...?	…の地図はありますか ...no chizu wa arimasu ka?
of the town	町の machi no
of the region	この地域の kono chiiki no
Can you show me where ... is on the map?	この地図で … はどこにありますか kono chizu de ... wa doko ni arimasu ka?

Do you have a ... in English?	英語の … はありますか eigo no ... wa arimasu ka?
a guidebook	ガイドブック gaidobukku
a leaflet	パンフレット panfuretto

Post office

郵便局 yuubinkyoku	post office
切手 kitte	stamps

Post office opening hours can vary but they are usually open from 9 am to 5 pm, Monday to Friday. Some post offices in the main cities stay open until around 7 pm and at weekends. You can withdraw money with your credit card or debit card issued outside Japan at post-office ATMs. A single transaction withdrawal is limited to 50,000 yen.

Where is the post office?	郵便局はどこですか yuubinkyoku wa doko desu ka?
Which is the counter...?	…カウンターはどこですか ...kauntaa wa doko desu ka?
for stamps	切手の kitte no

for parcels	小包の kozutsumi no
6 stamps for postcards...	…葉書用の切手6枚 ...hagaki-yoo no kitte roku-mai
first class post	速達 sokutatsu
for Britain	イギリスに igirisu ni
for America	アメリカに amerika ni
for Australia	オーストラリアに oosutoraria ni

Technology

メモリーカード memorii-kaado	memory card
デジカメ dejikame	digital camera
電子たばこ denshi-tabako	e-cigarette

Do you have batteries for this camera?	このカメラのバッテリーはありますか kono kamera no batterii wa arimasu ka?

Can you repair ...?	...を直せますか ...o naosemasu ka?
my screen	画面 gamen
my keypad	キーパッド kiipaddo
my lens	レンズ renzu
my charger	充電器 juudenki
I want to print my photos	写真を印刷したいんですが shashin o insatsu shitain desu ga
I have it on my USB	USBメモリーに入っています yuuesubii-memorii ni haitte imasu
I have it on my e-mail	メールに入っています meeru ni haitte imasu

Leisure

Sightseeing and tourist office

The Japan National Tourist Organisation has a great deal of information. Visit **www.jnto.go.jp**.

Where is the tourist office?	観光案内所はどこですか kankoo-annai-jo wa doko desu ka?
What can we visit in the area?	このエリアでは何を見ることができますか kono eria dewa nani o miru koto ga dekimasu ka?
Have you any leaflets?	何かパンフレットはありますか nani ka panfuretto wa arimasu ka?
Are there any excursions?	何か周遊ツアーはありますか nani ka shuuyuu tsuaa wa arimasu ka?
We'd like to go to...	… に行きたいです ... ni ikitai desu
How much does it cost to get in?	入るのにいくらかかりますか hairu noni ikura kakarimasu ka?

Are there reductions for...?	…の割引はありますか ...no waribiki wa arimasu ka?
children	子供 kodomo
students	学生 gakusei
over 60s	60歳以上 rokujussai-ijoo

Visiting Shinto shrines and Buddhist temples

All shrines have a **torii** (gate), which is the border between the sacred world and the secular world. The **temizuya** is a water pavilion, where you purify yourself. First, scoop up water in a ladle with your right hand and pour water over your left hand. Then hold the ladle with your left hand and wash your right hand. In your left hand, take some water poured from the ladle and rinse your mouth. At the altar, throw some coins into the offering box and ring the bells. Then bow twice, clap hands twice, then put your hands together and pray. At the end, you bow once.

There is not a strict temple etiquette as there is for shrines. At the **temizuya**, you can do the same as at a shrine. Throw coins into the offering box and pray silently; there is no need to clap.

Entertainment

Again, the Japan National Tourist Organisation website is very useful to see the type of events that are going on around Japan.

What is there to do in the evenings?	夜は何ができますか yoru wa nani ga dekimasu ka?
Do you have a programme of events?	イベントのプログラムはありますか ibento no puroguramu wa arimasu ka?
Is there anything for children?	子供のためのものはありますか kodomo no tame no mono wa arimasu ka?

Nightlife

Where can I go clubbing?	ナイトクラブはどこにありますか naitokurabu wa doko ni arimasu ka

bar	バー	baa
gay bar	ゲイバー	geibaa
gig	ギグ	gigu

music festival	ミュージックフェスティバル	myuujikku-fesutibaru
nightclub	ナイトクラブ	naitokurabu
party	パーティー	paatii
pub	居酒屋	izakaya

Leisure/interests

Where can I/ we go...?
…はどこでできますか
...wa doko de dekimasu ka?

fishing
釣り
tsuri

walking
散歩
sampo

Are there any good beaches near here?
この近くにいい浜辺はありますか
kono chikaku ni ii hamabe wa arimasu ka?

Is there a swimming pool?
スイミングプールはありますか
suimingu puuru wa arimasu ka?

adventure centre	アドベンチャーセンター	adobenchaa-sentaa
art gallery	美術館	bijutsukan

boat hire	貸しボート	kashi-booto
camping	キャンプ	kyanpu
museum	博物館	hakubutsukan
photography	写真	shashin
picnic area	ピクニック場	pikunikku-joo
piercing	ピアス	piasu
tattoo	入れ墨	irezumi
theme park	遊園地	yuuenchi
water park	親水公園	shinsuikooen
zoo	動物園	doobutsuen

YOU MAY HEAR...	
水泳禁止 suiei-kinshi	No swimming
飛び込み禁止 tobikomi-kinshi	No diving

Hot springs/public baths

A traditional leisure activity in Japan. You'll find separate baths for male and female guests. Each entrance has signs to indicate the following: male 男湯 (otoko-yu) and female 女湯 (onna-yu).

You cannot wear swimming costumes in the bath; clean your body using a basin before entering the bath tub. Japanese people love hot baths (around 40°C). You should not bring your towel into the tub; it's considered to be a 'communal' area.

Music

folk	フォーク	fooku
hip-hop	ヒップホップ	hippuhoppu
pop	ポップ	poppu
reggae	レゲー	regee
rock	ロック	rokku
techno	テクノ	tekuno

Are there any good concerts on?	何かいいコンサートはありますか nani ka ii konsaato wa arimasu ka?
Where can I/we get tickets for the concert?	コンサートのチケットはどこで買えますか konsaato no chiketto wa doko de kaemasu ka?
Where can I/we hear some classical/jazz music?	どこでクラッシック／ジャズを聴けますか doko de kurashikku/jazu o kikemasu ka?

Theatre/opera

Major hotels can get theatre and opera tickets for you, or you can buy them at ticket offices such as **Pureigaido** and **Midori no madoguchi** in stations and travel agencies. You can also buy tickets on the internet. If you are lucky enough to be able to obtain a **Kabuki** (Japanese theatre) ticket, it is definitely worth going. English translation is available.

General theatres/concert halls

S席 esu-seki	superior seat
A席 ee-seki	class A seat
B席 bii-seki	class B seat

Kabuki theatres

一等 ittoo	first class seat
二等 nitoo	second class seat
三階A sangai ee	second floor seat
桟敷 sajiki	circle
席 seki	seat
クローク kurooku	cloakroom

What is on at the theatre?	劇場では何をやっていますか gekijoo dewa nani o yatte imasu ka?
I'd like two tickets...	…のチケットを2枚ください ...no chiketto o ni-mai kudasai
for tonight	今夜の kon'ya no
for tomorrow night	明日の夜の ashita no yoru no

YOU MAY HEAR...	
もう開演していますので入場できません moo kaien shite imasu node nyuujoo dekimasen	You can't go in as the performance has started
休憩のときに入場できます kyuukei no toki ni nyuujoo dekimasu	You may enter at the interval

Cherry blossom viewing 花見 Hanami

Japanese people really appreciate cherry blossoms. They bloom in the middle of March in southern Japan, and at the beginning of May in Hokkaido. The blossom forecast (**sakura-zensen**) is even announced each year by the weather bureau. Families, friends or colleagues gather under the cherry trees and enjoy the beauty of the flowers with food and drink.

Sport

Where can we...?	…はどこでできますか ...wa doko de dekimasu ka?	
go swimming	水泳 suiei	
go jogging	ジョギング jogingu	

cycling	サイクリング	saikuringu
dancing	ダンス	dansu
kayaking	カヤック	kayakku
rock climbing	ロッククライミング	rokku-kuraimingu
snowboarding	スノーボード	sunooboodo
volleyball	バレーボール	bareebooru
water-skiing	ウォーター スキー	wootaasukii
windsurfing	ウインドサーフィン	uindosaafin

Do I have to be a member?	会員にならなくてはいけませんか kaiin ni naranakute wa ikemasen ka?

Leisure

How much is it per hour?	1時間いくらですか ichi-jikan ikura desu ka?
Can we hire...?	…を借りられますか ...o kariraremasu ka?
rackets	ラケット raketto
golf clubs	ゴルフクラブ gorufukurabu
I want to try...	...をしてみたいんですが ...o shite mitaindesu ga
I've never done this before	今までやったことがありません ima made yatta koto ga arimasen
Where can I/we get tickets for the game?	どこで試合のチケットを買えますか doko de shiai no chiketto o kaemasu ka?
I want to hire skis	スキー板を借りたいです sukii ita o karitai desu
Does the price include...?	…の値段は含まれていますか ...no nedan wa fukumarete imasu ka?
boots	ブーツ buutsu
poles	ストック sutokku

What time is the last lift?	最後の上りのリフトは何時ですか saigo no nobori no rifuto wa nan-ji desu ka?
Can you adjust my bindings?	締め具を調節してもらえますか shimegu o choosetsu shite moraemasu ka?
Have you ever skied before?	今までにスキーをしたことはありますか ima made ni sukii o shita koto wa arimasu ka?
What is your boot size?	ブーツのサイズはいくつですか buutsu no saizu wa ikutsu desu ka?
Do you want skiing lessons?	スキーレッスンを受けたいですか sukii ressun o uketai desu ka?

クロスカントリースキー kurosukantorii sukii	cross-country skiing
リフト券 rifuto ken	ski pass

Walking

Do you know any good walks?	何かいいウォーキングコースはありますか nanika ii wookingu koosu wa arimasu ka?
How many kilometres is the walk?	ウォーキングコースは何キロですか wookingu koosu wa nan kiro desu ka?
Is there a map of the walk?	ウォーキングコースの地図はありますか wookingu koosu no chizu wa arimasu ka?
Do you have a detailed map of the area?	この付近の詳しい地図がありますか kono fukin no kuwashii chizu ga arimasu ka?

Communications

Telephone and mobile

You can make an international call from a grey public telephone. Some green phones are only for domestic calls. Check if the sign states whether it has the option for international calls 国際電話 (kokusai denwa). You can use 100 yen coins or buy a telephone card from a vending machine. Be wary when purchasing a card as there are various types available and the most common cards are for local and national calls only. If you use your mobile phone in Japan, it could be very expensive. Check with your provider before travelling.

テレホンカード terehon-kaado	phonecard
公衆電話 kooshuu denwa	public phone
携帯 (電話) keitai (denwa)	mobile

I want to make a phone call — 電話をかけたいです denwa o kaketai desu

Where can I buy a phonecard?	どこでテレホンカードを買えますか doko de terehon-kaado o kaemasu ka?
for ... yen	…円分 ...en bun
What is your mobile number?	携帯 (電話) は何番ですか keitai (denwa) wa namban desu ka?
My mobile number is...	私の携帯 (電話) は … 番です watashi no keitai (denwa) wa ... ban desu
smartphone	スマホ sumaho
charger	充電器 juudenki
Do you have a ... charger/cable?	…の充電器／充電ケーブルはありますか ...no juudenki/juuden-keeburu wa arimasu ka?
I have an e-ticket on my phone	eチケットは携帯に入っています ii-chiketto wa keitai ni haitte imasu
I need to phone a UK/US/Australian number	イギリス／アメリカ／オーストラリアに電話しなければいけないんですが igirisu/amerika/oosutoraria ni denwa shinakereba ikenain desu ga

YOU MAY HEAR...
もしもし moshimoshi Hello
…さん、お願いします ...san, onegai shimasu I'd like to speak to..., please
どちらさまですか dochirasama desu ka? Who's calling?
アンジェラです anjera desu It's Angela
少々お待ちください… shooshoo omachi kudasai... Just a moment...

Can I speak to...?	…さん、おねがいします ...san, onegai shimasu?
I'll call back later	後でかけ直します ato de kakenaoshimasu
This is Mr.../Mrs...	…です ...desu
How do I get an outside line?	外線はどうやって使いますか gaisen wa dooyatte tsukaimasu ka?

YOU MAY HEAR...	
お話中です (o)hanashi-chuu desu	The line is engaged
またおかけ直しください mata okakenaoshi kudasai	Please try later
メッセージを残しますか messeeji o nokoshimasu ka?	Do you want to leave a message?
アナウンスの後にメッセージを残してください anaunsu no ato ni messeeji o nokoshite kudasa	Leave a message after the tone

Please switch off all mobile phones — 携帯電話の電源を切ってください
keitai-denwa no dengen o kitte kudasai

Messaging

SMS is not as popular in Japan as it is in other countries, but sending emails to mobile phones is.

I will text you — メッセージを送ります
messeeji o okurimasu

Can you text me? 私にメッセージを送ってもらえますか
watashi ni messeeji o okutte moraemasu ka?

e-mail メール
meeru

to send an e-mail めーるを送ります
meeru o okurimasu

What is your e-mail address? メールアドレスは何ですか
meeru adoresu wa nan desu ka?

How do you spell it? それはどう書きますか
sore wa doo kakimasu ka?

All one word 一語です
ichigo desu

My e-mail address is... 私のメールアドレスは … です
watashi no meeru adoresu wa ... desu

clare.smith@bit.co.uk clare ドット smith アットマーク bit ドット co ドット uk
shii eru ee aaru ii dotto esu emu ai ti eichi attomaaku bii ai tii dotto shii oo dotto yuu kei

Can I send an e-mail? メールを送ることはできますか
meeru o okuru koto wa dekimasu ka?

Internet

Internet cafés are still very common, unlike in the UK. People go there to watch videos, play computer games and read magazines, as well as using the computer. Computer and internet terminology tends to be in English.

Are there any internet cafés here?	この辺りにインターネットカフェはありますか kono atari ni intaanetto kafe wa arimasu ka?
How much is it to log on for an hour?	１時間いくらですか ichi-jikan ikura desu ka?
Wi-Fi	WiFi waifai
social network	ソーシャルネットワーク soosharu-nettowaaku
app	アプリ apuri
laptop	ラップトップ rapputoppu
tablet	タブレット taburetto

What is the Wi-Fi password?	WiFiのパスワードは何ですか waifai no pasuwaado wa nan desu ka?
Do you have free Wi-Fi?	無料のWiFiはありますか muryoo no waifai wa arimasu ka?
Can I borrow your...?	...を貸してもらえませんか ...o kashite moraemasen ka?
Add me on Facebook	Facebookで友だちになってください feesubukku de tomodachi ni natte kudasai
Is there 3G/4G signal?	3G/4Gにつながりますか surii-gii/foo-gii ni tsunagarimasu ka?
I need to access my webmail	メールをコンピュータでチェックしなければいけないんですが meeru o konpyuuta de chekku shinakereba ikenain desu ga
I would like to use Skype	スカイプを使いたいんですが sukaipu o tsukaitain desu ga

Practicalities

Money

ATM opening hours vary depending on location and the providing bank. Japan still mainly operates on cash but many large shops, hotels and restaurants will accept cards. Not all cash machines will accept non-Japanese cards for withdrawing cash. Check if the machine has an 'International ATM Service' symbol. You can withdraw cash at post-office ATMs too, but it is easiest to change/withdraw yen at the airport or in big cities.

クレジットカード kurejitto kaado	credit card
現金引き出し機/ATM genkin hikidashi ki/ee-tii-emu	cash machine
領収書 ryooshuusho	till receipt
両替率 ryoogae-ritsu	exchange rate

Where can I change some money?	どこでお金を両替できますか doko de okane o ryoogae dekimasu ka?
When does the bank open?	いつ銀行は開きますか itsu ginkoo wa akimasu ka?
When does the bank close?	いつ銀行は閉まりますか itsu ginkoo wa shimarimasu ka?
Can I pay with...?	…で払えますか ...de haraemasu ka?
yen	円 en
dollar	ドル doru
pound	ポンド pondo
Where is the nearest cash machine?	最寄のATMはどこですか moyori no ee-tii-emu wa doko desu ka?
Can I use my credit card at the cash machine?	このATMで私のクレジットカードは使えますか kono ee-tii-emu de watashi no kurejitto kaado wa tsukaemasu ka?
What is the exchange rate for...?	...の両替率はいくらですか ...no ryoogae-ritsu wa ikura desu ka?
Do you have any loose change?	小銭は持っていますか kozeni wa motte imasu ka?

Paying

現金のみ genkin-nomi	cash only
お金をおろす okane o orosu	to withdraw money
デビットカード debitto-kaado	debit card
クレジットカード kurejitto-kaado	credit card
コンタクトレス払い kontakutoresu-barai	contactless payment

How much is it?	いくらですか ikura desu ka?
Can I pay by...?	…で払えますか ...de haraemasu ka?
credit card	クレジットカード kurejitto kaado
Is service included?	サービス料は含まれていますか saabisu-ryoo wa fukumarete imasu ka?
Is tax included?	税金は含まれていますか zeikin wa fukumarete imasu ka?

Can I pay by card?	カードで払えますか kaado de haraemasuka?
Where is the nearest cash machine?	一番近いATMはどこですか ichiban chikai eetiiemu wa doko desu ka?
Is there a credit card charge?	クレジットカードで払うと手数料がかかりますか kurejitto-kaado de harau to tesuuryoo ga kakarimasu ka?
Is there a discount for senior citizens?	シニア割引はありますか shinia waribiki wa arimasu ka?
Can you write down the price?	値段を書いてもらえませんか nedan o kaite moraemasen ka?
Where do I pay?	どこで支払いますか doko de shiharaimasu ka?
I need a receipt, please	領収書をください ryooshuusho o kudasai
Do I pay in advance?	前払いですか maebarai desu ka?
Do I need to pay a deposit?	手付金は必要ですか tetsukekin wa hitsuyoo desu ka?
I've nothing smaller	細かいお金を持っていません komakai okane o motte imasen
(no change)	小銭がありません kozeni ga arimasen

YOU MAY HEAR...	
消費税込みです shoohizei komi desu	Consumer tax is included
消費税は含まれていますが、サービス料は別です shoohizei wa fukumarete imasu ga, saabisuryoo wa betsu desu	Consumer tax is included but not a service charge
レジで支払ってください reji de shiharatte kudasai	Pay at the till

Luggage

My luggage hasn't arrived — 私の荷物が届いていません
watashi no nimotsu ga todoite imasen

My suitcase has been damaged on the flight — 私のスーツケースが飛行中に壊れてしまいました
watashi no suutsukeesu ga hikoochuu ni kowarete shimaimashita

手荷物 tenimotsu	baggage reclaim

携帯品一時預かり所 keitai-hin ichiji azukari-sho	left-luggage office
手荷物カート tenimotsu kaato	luggage trolley

Repairs

This is broken	これは壊れています kore wa kowarete imasu
Is it worth repairing?	直す価値はありますか naosu kachi wa arimasu ka?
Can you repair...?	…は直せますか ...wa naosemasu ka?
this	これ kore
these shoes	この靴 kono kutsu
my watch	私の時計 watashi no tokei

YOU MAY HEAR...	
申し訳ありませんが、直すことはできません mooshiwake arimasen ga, naosu koto wa dekimasen	Sorry, but we can't mend it

Laundry

ドライクリーニング dorai kuriiningu	dry-cleaner's
洗剤 senzai	soap powder
漂白剤 hyoohaku zai	bleach
洗濯機 sentakuki	washing machine

Where can I wash these clothes?	この衣類はどこで洗えますか kono irui wa doko de araemasu ka?
Where is the nearest launderette?	最寄のコインランドリーはどこですか moyori no koin randorii wa doko desu ka?

Complaints

The ... does/ do not work (for machines)	…が動きません ...ga ugokimasen
heating	暖房機 dambooki
air conditioning	エアコン eakon

The ... is/are dirty	…が汚れています ...ga yogorete imasu
toilet	トイレ toire
sheets	シーツ shiitsu
The light is not working	電気がつきません denki ga tsukimasen
I want a refund	払い戻ししてください haraimodoshi shite kudasai

Problems

Can you help me?	助けてもらえますか tasukete moraemasu ka?
I speak very little Japanese	私は少ししか日本語が話せません watashi wa sukoshi shika nihongo ga hanasemasen
Does anyone here speak English?	誰か英語が話せる人はいますか dareka eigo ga hanaseru hito wa imasu ka?
What's the matter?	どうしましたか doo shimashita ka?

I would like to speak to whoever is in charge	担当者と話したいんですが tantoosha to hanashitain desu ga
I'm lost	道に迷いました michi ni mayoimashita
I missed my...	…に遅れてしまいました ...ni okurete shimaimashita
train	電車 densha
plane	飛行機 hikooki
connection	乗り継ぎ noritsugi
The coach has left without me	バスが出てしまいました basu ga dete shimaimashita
Can you show me how this works please?	どうやって使うのかやってみせてもらえませんか dooyatte tsukau no ka yatte misete moraemasen ka?
I have lost my money	お金をなくしてしまいました okane o nakushite shimaimashita
I need to get to...	…に行かなくてはいけないんです ...ni ikanakute wa ikenain desu
Where can I recycle this?	これはどこでリサイクルできますか kore wa doko de risaikuru dekimasu ka?

I need to access my online banking	ネットバンキングをしなければいけないんですが netto-bankingu o shinakereba ikenain desu ga
Do you have wheelchairs?	車いすはありますか kurumaisu wa arimasu ka?
Where is the wheelchair-accessible entrance?	車いす用の出入り口はどこですか kurumaisu-yoo no deiriguchi wa doko desu ka?
Do you have an induction loop?	誘導ループシステムはありますか yuudoo ruupu shisutemu wa arimasu ka?
Do you have any bedrooms on the ground floor?	一階の部屋はありますか ikkai no heya wa arimasu ka?
Where is the lift?	エレベーターはどこにありますか erebeetaa wa doko ni arimasu ka?
Can you visit ... in a wheelchair?	…は車いすでも行けますか ...wa kurumaisu demo ikemasu ka?

Emergencies

There are two emergency numbers in Japan:
Police **110**
Ambulance/Fire **119**

医者　isha	doctor
救急車　kyuukyuusha	ambulance
警察　keisatsu	police
消防士　shooboshi	firemen
警察署　keisatsu-sho	police station
交番　kooban	police box (small neighbourhood police station)

Help!	助けて tasukete!
Fire!	火事だ kaji da!
Can you help me?	助けてもらえますか tasukete moraemasu ka?
There's been an accident!	事故があった jiko ga atta!
Someone has been injured	ケガをした人がいます kega o shita hito ga imasu

Please call...	…を呼んでください ...o yonde kudasai
Where is the police station?	警察署はどこですか keisatsu-sho wa doko desu ka?
I've been...	私は… watashi wa...
robbed	泥棒にあいました doroboo ni aimashita
attacked	襲われました osowaremashita
Someone has stolen...	誰かに … を盗られました dareka ni ... o toraremashita
my bag	かばん no kaban
my money	お金 okane
My car has been broken into	車を壊されました kuruma o kowasaremashita
I've been raped	私は暴行を受けました watashi wa bookoo o ukemashita
I want to speak to a policewoman	女性の警察官と話がしたいです josei no keisatsukan to hanashi ga shitai desu

I need to make a telephone call	電話をかけなければいけません denwa o kakenakereba ikemasen
I need a report for my insurance	保険のための報告書をもらえますか hoken no tame no hookoku-sho o moraemasu ka
How much is the fine?	罰金はいくらですか bakkin wa ikura desu ka?
Where do I pay it?	どこで払いますか doko de haraimasu ka?

Health

Pharmacy

A pharmacy can usually be found in major department stores and supermarkets. There are many pharmacies, which sell a variety of items including medicine, cosmetics, and snacks.

薬局 yakkyoku	pharmacy/chemist

Summertime is very humid and hot. If you go outside, you should drink plenty of water to prevent heatstroke 熱中症 (netchuushoo). Tap water is safe to drink in Japan.

Another problem in summer is the mosquitoes. You can buy a repellent 虫よけ (mushi-yoke) and an anti-itching cream かゆみ止め (kayumidome) from a pharmacy.

Can you give me something for...?	…に効く薬をもらえませんか ...ni kiku kusuri o moraemasen ka?

a headache	頭痛 zutsuu
car sickness	車酔い kuruma yoi
a cough	咳 seki
diarrhoea	下痢 geri
Is it safe for children?	これは子供にも安全ですか kore wa kodomo nimo anzen desu ka?
How much should I give him?	どれだけ飲ませればいいですか doredake nomasereba ii desu ka?

YOU MAY HEAR...	
1日に3回… ichinichi ni sankai...	Three times a day...
…ご飯 ...gohan	...meals
食前 shokuzen	before meals
食中 shokuchuu	with meals
食後 shokugo	after meals

asthma	喘息	zensoku
condom	コンドーム	kondoomu
contact lenses	コンタクトレンズ	kontakuto-renzu

inhaler	吸入器	kyuunyuuki
morning-after pill	モーニングアフターピル	mooningu-afutaa-piru
mosquito bite	蚊に刺されました	ka ni sasaremashita
painkillers	痛み止め	itamidome
period	生理	seiri
the Pill	ピル	piru
tampon	タンポン	tanpon

Body

In Japanese the possessive (my, his, her, etc.) is not generally used when referring to parts of the body, for example:

I've broken my leg	ashi o otte shimaimashita
Mr Tanaka hurt his arm	tanaka-san wa ude o itamete shimaimashita

arm	腕	ude
chest	胸	mune
ear	耳	mimi
eye	目	me
finger	指	yubi

foot	足	ashi
hand	手	te
head	頭	atama
heart	心臓	shinzoo
leg	足	ashi
lower back	腰	koshi
neck	首	kubi
toe	足の指	ashi no yubi
tooth	歯	ha
upper back	背中	senaka
wrist	手首	tekubi

Doctor

病院 byooin	hospital
救急 kyuukyuu	emergency

FACE TO FACE

具合が悪いです
guai ga warui desu
I feel ill

熱はありますか
netsu wa arimasu ka?
Do you have a temperature?

いいえ、…が痛いです
iie, ...ga itai desu
No, I have a pain in my...

I need a doctor	医者にかかりたいです isha ni kakaritai desu
I'm diabetic	私は糖尿病です watashi wa toonyoobyoo desu
I'm pregnant	私は妊娠しています watashi wa ninshin shite imasu
I'm on the pill	ピルを飲んでいます piru o nonde imasu
I'm allergic to penicillin	ペニシリンのアレルギーがあります penishirin no arerugii ga arimasu
Will I have to pay?	お金を払わなければいけませんか okane o harawanakereba ikemasen ka?
How much will it cost?	いくらかかりますか ikura kakarimasu ka?

Can you give me a receipt for the insurance?	保険のための領収書をもらえますか hoken no tame no ryooshuusho o moraemasu ka?
antibiotics	抗生物質 koosei-busshitsu
cystitis	膀胱炎 bookooen
drug abuse	麻薬の乱用 mayaku no ran'yoo
epilepsy	てんかん tankan
food poisoning	食中毒 shokuchuudoku
headache	頭痛 zutsuu
sprain	ねんざ nenza
STI or STD (sexually transmitted infection/disease)	性病 seibyoo
GP (general practitioner)	医者 isha
A&E (accident and emergency)	救急病院 kyuukyuu-byooin

I've run out of medication	薬が終わってしまいました kusuri ga owatte shimaimashita
I'm allergic to...	...にアレルギーがあります ...ni arerugii ga arimasu
animal hair	動物の毛 doobutsu no ke
dairy	乳製品 nyuuseihin
gluten	グルテン guruten
nuts	ナッツ nattsu
pollen	花粉 kafun
I have a prescription for...	...の処方薬を持っています ...no shohooyaku o motte imasu
I have a ... intolerance	...の過敏症です ...no kabinshoo desu
I take (illegal) drugs	麻薬を使っています mayaku o tsukatte imasu

YOU MAY HEAR...	
あなたは病院に行かなければいけません anata wa byooin ni ikanakereba ikemasen	You will have to go to hospital
大したことはありません taishita koto wa arimasen	It's not serious

Do not drink alcohol	アルコールを飲まないでください arukooru o nomanaide kudasai

Do you drink?	お酒を飲みますか osake o nomimasu ka?
Do you smoke?	タバコを吸いますか tabako o suimasu ka?
Do you take drugs?	麻薬を使っています mayaku o tsukatte imasu?
Are you taking any medication?	なにか薬を飲んでいますか nanika kusuri o nonde imasu ka?

Dentist

I need a dentist	歯医者にかかりたいです haisha ni kakaritai desu
I have a toothache	歯が痛いです ha ga itai desu
Can you do a temporary filling?	仮の詰め物はできますか kari no tsumemono wa dekimasu ka?
It hurts	痛いです itai desu
Can you give me something for the pain?	何か痛みに効く薬はありますか nanika itami ni kiku kusuri wa arimasu ka?
Can you repair my dentures?	義歯を治してもらえますか gishi o naoshite moraemasu ka?

YOU MAY HEAR...	
抜かなければいけません nukanakereba ikemasen	I'll have to take it out
詰め物が必要です tsumemono ga hitsuyoo desu	You need a filling
少し痛むかもしれません sukoshi itamu kamo shiremasen	This might hurt a little

Eating out

Food in Japan

All types of eating places and food can be found in Japan. Except for in hotel restaurants and up-market traditional Japanese restaurants, which usually have set dining times, you can have your meal at any time throughout the day. American-style fast food is popular and there are family restaurants that cater for this. There are also many specialized restaurants where only one type of food is served, for example, **soba-ya** (Japanese noodle shop), **raamen-ya** (Chinese noodle shop), **sushi-ya** (sushi restaurant), **tonkatsu-ya** (pork cutlet restaurant) and even **unagi-ya** (BBQ eel restaurant). Visit the Food and Drink page on **www.japan-guide.com** for a guide to eating out in Japan.

Most coffee shops and restaurants will automatically bring you a glass of tap water (which is safe to drink) and **oshibori**, a small, damp hand towel to wipe your hands. In traditional Japanese restaurants you will find low tables and (often) **tatami matting**, which is a traditional Japanese mat made of straw. These restaurants require you to remove your shoes, so make sure your socks are respectable. Many eating places in Japan have plates of plastic food on display to show customers what they offer.

You say **itadakimasu** (I humbly eat) before a meal and **gochisoosama deshita** (it was a good meal) afterwards.

In Japanese restaurants, a spoon is normally not offered. To eat soup, you pick up the bowl with one hand and sip from the edge of the bowl. Use chopsticks to pick up other ingredients.

Bill and charges

Consumer tax is currently at 8% but there are plans to increase this to 10% during 2017. However, this date is still to be decided. A service charge of 10% is generally included in the bill and tipping is not customary.

The word for the bill is **(o)kanjoo**. You can ask for the bill by saying '(o)kanjoo onegai shimasu'.

Coffee shops 喫茶店 (kissaten)

Coffee shops serve non-alcoholic drinks and many

of them also serve foods such as salads, sandwiches, pasta dishes and rice dishes. It is fun to find a good 'morning service', which includes a small complimentary breakfast when you order a coffee or tea. Ask for **mooningu setto** (literally a 'morning set'). If you would like to order tea with milk, be sure to specify **miruku tii**, as otherwise you will probably be served a lemon tea.

Noodle shops 蕎麦屋 (soba-ya)/うどん屋 (udon-ya)/ラーメン屋 (raamen-ya)

Noodles are Japanese fast food. There are three popular types of noodles in Japan. These are **soba**, **udon** and **raamen**. **Soba** (buckwheat noodles) and **udon** (white flour noodles) are both traditional Japanese noodles. You can choose different toppings such as chicken or tempura. **Raamen** originated from China but has gained huge popularity amongst all generations in Japan. It comes in hot soup or is served cold without soup, in summer.

Sushi shops 鮨屋 (sushi-ya)

There are a number of different **sushi** types but the most popular are **nigiri-zushi** (a rice ball shaped in the palm of the hand with raw fish on top), and **temaki-zushi** (rice and raw fish often wrapped in a cone shape with a seaweed sheet wrapper). **Toro**, a fatty part of tuna, is also very popular. Although generally **sushi** is expensive, you can find good deals at lunch time or at very cheap and decent quality 'rotating' (kaiten) sushi shops where you can see the sushi and pick what you fancy. One plate usually costs between 100 and 300 yen.

Tempura shops 天麩羅屋 (tempura-ya)

Tempura is a deep fried dish of vegetables and seafood in light batter. It was originally introduced by the Portuguese. Some shops prepare **tempura** in front of you and serve it in a very elegant manner.

Pubs 居酒屋 (izakaya)

Izakaya are very good places to try out a range of Japanese food and drink. They serve cheap but very tasty food in small portions similar to Spanish tapas, and usually have a large selection to choose from. Amongst these, **yakitori** (BBQ chicken), **agedashi-dofu** (deep-fried bean curd) and **sashimi** (sliced raw fish) are all worth trying.

Vending machines 自動販売機 (jidoo-hambaiki)

Vending machines contain all kinds of hot and cold drinks as well as snacks. Notes can be used in the machines.

Convenience stores コンビニ (kombini)

If you need a late-night snack or don't want to go to a restaurant, a convenience store is a good place to stock up on food. Sandwiches, salads, pot noodles, and so on are all available to buy. You may also come across rice balls, which have various fillings such as tuna-mayo (tsuna mayo) and salmon (sake). You may also want to try a **bento**. The staff will heat up **obento** (packed lunchbox), soup and other dishes for you.

Department stores デパート (depaato)

Most department stores have a designated restaurant floor (usually on the top floor) where you will find various types of restaurants, including western-style places. Department store basement floors have good delis and take-away food.

Lunchboxes お弁当 (obento)

Obento is a pre-packed lunchbox. You can buy various types from department stores, convenience stores, supermarkets and even train stations. Many train stations sell specialised lunchboxes prepared with local delicacies such as dimsum lunchbox in Yokohama, tempura riceballs in Nagoya, BBQ eel in Hamamatsu and trout sushi in Toyama.

In a bar/café

FACE TO FACE

ご注文は
gochuumon wa?
May I have your order?

ミルクティーをお願いします
miruku tii o onegai shimasu
A tea with milk, please

a coffee	コーヒー koohii
a lager	ビール biiru
no sugar	砂糖なしで satoo nashi de
for two	二人に futari ni
for me	私に watashi ni
for him/her	彼/彼女に kare/kanojo ni
for us	私たちに watashi-tachi ni

with ice	氷を入れて koori o irete
a bottle of mineral water	ミネラルウォーター一本 mineraru wootaa ippon
sparkling	炭酸水 tansansui

Other drinks to try

Iced coffee アイスコーヒー aisukoohii is very popular in Japan.

Japanese tea お茶 ocha is usually served with your meal for free in Japanese restaurants, including Japanese noodle shops. You can buy chilled or hot canned tea from vending machines. There are many kinds to choose from.

Matcha green tea 抹茶 maccha is the tea used at tea ceremonies and is rather bitter, but a sweet iced green tea is available in some coffee shops. Green tea ice cream is a popular favourite.

Japanese rice wine 酒 sake can be drunk either chilled or warmed. There are different degrees of sweetness and lots of local ones, which are called 地酒 jizake.

焼酎 shoochuu is Japanese vodka. It is cheap and again there are many local varieties.

チュウハイ chuuhai is a mixture of shoochuu and lemonade (or other juices) which is popular among young people.

梅酒 umeshu is a smooth and sweet Japanese plum wine.

Menu reader

Reading the menu

Although traditional Japanese cuisine, **kaiseki-ryoori**, has a long list of dishes (which is usually a set menu), most Japanese restaurants, unlike western restaurants, do not have starters or main meals. Below are sample menus for some popular eating places.

General Japanese restaurant

You'll often find a set meal (定食 teishoku), which is a main dish with a bowl of rice, soup, and a side dish all served together on a tray.

Table top cooking restaurant

鉄板焼き teppan-yaki meat, seafood and vegetables cooked on a table-top hot plate

すき焼き suki-yaki sliced beef, bean curd, mushrooms and other vegetables cooked in a soy sauce-based sauce

しゃぶしゃぶ shabu-shabu thinly sliced beef dipped and cooked quickly in a hot stock, eaten with sesame seed, soy sauce and Japanese lime-based dip

Izakaya

居酒屋 Izakaya is a casual eating and drinking place. Many people go there after work. The dishes are generally small and inexpensive. A small appetizer called お通し (otooshi) will come with your first drink order. This will be automatically included in your bill at a few hundred yen as an entry fee.

A typical Izakaya menu for food and drink is shown below, in various categories.

Beef 牛肉 (gyuu-niku)

牛丼 gyuu-don sliced beef cooked with soy sauce on rice

牛肉たたき gyuu-niku tataki seared sliced beef served with ginger

牛刺し gyuu-sashi sliced raw beef

ハンバーグ hambaagu hamburger steak

ハンバーガー hambaagaa hamburger

串かつ kushi-katsu crumbed meat and vegetables, deep-fried on skewers

肉じゃが nikujaga sliced beef cooked with potato in a soy sauce-based stock

レバー rebaa grilled or pan-fried liver

しゃぶしゃぶ shabushabu thinly sliced beef cooked quickly at the table in boiling stock

すきやき suki-yaki sliced beef with vegetables and raw egg, cooked at the table

ステーキ suteeki steak

焼き肉 yaki-niku grilled sliced beef

Chicken 鶏肉 (tori-niku)

から揚げ karaage deep-fried chicken coated in mild spice and herbs

ねぎま negima char-grilled skewered chicken and spring onion

竜田揚げ tatta-age deep-fried marinated (soy sauce, sake, ginger) chicken

照り焼きチキン teriyaki-chikin pan-fried chicken in teriyaki sauce (soy sauce and rice wine)

つくね tsukune minced chicken ball char-grilled and coated with soy sauce

焼き鳥 yaki-tori char-grilled skewered chicken

Pork 豚肉 (buta-niku)

豚肉の生姜焼き buta-niku no shooga yaki pan-fried thinly sliced pork with soy sauce and ginger

餃子 gyooza **fried pork dumpling**

かつ丼 katsudon **deep-fried, bread-crumbed pork cutlet on rice**

かつカレー katsu-karee **deep-fried, bread-crumbed pork and curry on rice**

とんかつ tonkatsu **deep-fried, bread-crumbed pork cutlet**

焼き豚/チャーシュー yakibuta/chaashuu **sliced roast pork**

Fish 魚 (sakana) and other seafood dishes

刺身 sashimi **sliced raw fish**

焼き魚 yaki-zakana **grilled fish**

煮魚 ni-zakana **simmered fish**

エビフライ ebi-furai **deep-fried, crumbed prawn**

えび天ぷら ebi-tempura **deep-fried prawn in light batter topped on rice**

かきフライ kaki-furai **deep-fried, crumbed oyster**

かにすき kanisuki **hotpot dish with crab**

かに酢 (の物) kanisu (nomono) **crab meat in white rice vinegar**

かつおたたき katsuo tataki **seared bonito with grated ginger**

いかの姿焼き ika no sugata-yaki **whole grilled squid**

いわしの生姜煮 iwashi no shooga-ni **simmered gingered sardine**

さばの塩焼き saba no shioyaki salt-grilled mackerel

さばの味噌煮 saba no misoni simmered mackerel in miso sauce

さばの竜田揚げ saba no tatta-age deep-fried marinated (soy sauce, sake, ginger) mackerel

さんまの塩焼き samma no shioyaki salt-grilled (Pacific) saury

酢牡蛎 sugaki fresh oyster in vinegar

刺身盛り合わせ sashimi moriawase assorted sliced raw fish

たこ焼き takoyaki octopus cooked in a dough ball

たらの味噌焼き tara no miso yaki grilled cod with soy bean paste

てっさ tessa thinly sliced raw puffer fish (prepared by a licensed chef)

うな重 unajuu/うな丼 unadon grilled eel on rice

Vegetables 野菜 (yasai)

揚げだし豆腐 agedashi-doofu deep-fried bean curd

ふろふきだいこん furoruki daikon simmered Japanese radish with sauce

冷奴 hiyayakko cold bean curd

ほうれん草おひたし hoorensoo ohitashi cooked spinach with sesame seeds

かぼちゃの煮物 kabocha no nimono simmered pumpkin

きんぴらごぼう kimpira goboo **shaved burdock root, pan-fried with soy sauce and chilli**

こんにゃく konnyaku **hard, jelly like product made from root vegetables**

きゅうりの酢の物 kyuuri no su no mono **sliced cucumber in vinegar**

のり nori **dried seaweed sheet**

納豆 nattoo **fermented soy beans**

ポテトフライ poteto furai **chips**

白和え shiraae **boiled vegetables mixed with bean curd**

漬物 tsukemono **pickled vegetables**

わかめの酢の物 wakame no suno mono **seaweed in vinegar**

焼きなす yakinasu **grilled aubergine**

焼きしいたけ yaki-shiitake **grilled Japanese shiitake-mushroom**

野菜天ぷら yasai tempura **deep-fried vegetables in light batter**

Rice ご飯 (gohan) and other mains

おでん oden **various vegetables, bean curd and skewered beef tendon cooked in stock**

お好み焼き okonomi-yaki **Japanese style pizza**

そば soba **thin, brown, buckwheat noodles**

うどん udon thick, white, wheat flour noodles

ラーメン raamen Chinese style noodles

カレー karee curry (and rice)

かつカレー katsu-karee bread-crumbed, deep-fried pork on curry and rice

かつ丼 katsu-don crumbed, deep-fried pork, egg and onion cooked with soy sauce on rice

天丼 tendon deep-fried prawn in light batter on rice

牛丼 gyuudon sliced beef, onion and egg cooked with soy sauce on rice

スパゲティー supagetii spaghetti

ピザ piza pizza

雑炊 zoosui Japanese savoury rice porridge with egg

鮭茶漬け sake-chazuke Japanese tea poured over rice, flaked salmon and seaweed

お茶漬け o-chazuke Japanese tea poured over rice

おにぎり onigiri rice ball wrapped with seaweed sheet

焼き飯 yakimeshi Japanese-style fried rice

チャーハン chaahan Chinese-style fried rice

Soup 汁 (shiru)

豆腐の味噌汁 toofu no misoshiru soy bean paste-based soup with soy bean curd

わかめの味噌汁 wakame no misoshiru soy bean paste-based soup with seaweed

あげの味噌汁 age no misoshiru soy bean paste-based soup with fried bean curd sheet

雑煮 zooni soup with rice cake

すまし汁 sumashijiru clear soup

Drinks お飲み物 (o-nomimono)

ビール biiru lager beer

生ビール nama biiru draught beer

大瓶 oo-bin large bottle of lager

小瓶 ko-bin small bottle of lager

大ジョッキ dai-jokki large glass of lager (draught)

中ジョッキ chuu-jokki medium glass of lager (draught)

小ジョッキ shoo-jokki small glass of lager (draught)

酒 sake Japanese rice wine, warm or chilled

チュウハイ chuuhai Japanese vodka with lemonade (or another type of juice)

水割り mizu-wari whisky with water

コーラ koora cola

ジュース juusu juice

オレンジジュース orenji-juusu orange juice

お茶 o-cha Japanese tea. Traditionally in a sushi shop, tea is served after you finish the meal. This tea is called あがり agari.

水 mizu **water**

炭酸水 tansansui **sparkling water**

ミネラルウォーター mineraru wootaa **mineral water (still)**

コーヒー koohii **coffee**

紅茶 koocha **English tea**

Sushi shop

Sushi: normally means rice balls (**nigiri**) with sliced raw fish but there are various types.

にぎり(鮨) nigiri (zushi) **rice balls with sliced raw fish**

手巻き寿司 temaki-zushi **rolled sushi with seaweed sheet (without using bamboo mat)**

巻き寿司 maki-zushi **rolled sushi with seaweed sheet using bamboo mat**

細巻き hoso-maki **small rolled sushi**

太巻き futo-maki **large rolled sushi with cooked egg, vegetable, mushroom, fish**

いなり寿司 inari-zushi **seasoned rice, wrapped in fried thin bean curd**

カッパ (巻き) kappa (maki) **small rolled sushi with cucumber**

盛り合わせ moriawase **assorted sushi**

For **nigiri** and **temaki**, you can choose what to put on/in from below:

あまえび amaebi sweet shrimps

赤貝 akagai ark shell (red shellfish)

穴子 anago conger eel (usually grilled)

あわび awabi abalone

えび ebi prawn

貝 kai shellfish

かに kani crab

かつお katsuo bonito

ひらめ hirame plaice

ホタテ hotate scallop

いか ika squid

いくら ikura salmon roe

いわし iwashi sardine

まぐろ maguro tuna

さば saba mackerel

鯛 tai snapper

たこ tako octopus

うなぎ unagi eel (usually grilled)

うに uni sea urchin

卵 tamago sliced, flavoured egg omelette

Soup and sides

味噌汁 misoshiru **soy bean paste-based soup**

すまし汁 sumashi-jiru **soy sauce-based clear soup**

茶碗蒸し chawan-mushi **steamed flavoured egg with vegetable, chicken, mushroom and prawn**

だし巻き卵 dashimaki tamago **rolled flavoured eggs**

わさび wasabi **Japanese green horseradish**

がり gari **thinly sliced, pickled ginger**

Noodle shop

そば soba **thin, brown, buckwheat noodles**

うどん udon **thick, white, wheat flour noodles**

そうめん soomen **thin, white, wheat flour cold noodles**

ラーメン raamen **Chinese style noodles**

Udon and Soba

釜揚げうどん kamaage udon **warm/cold udon with dipping sauce**

カレーうどん/そば karee udon/soba **udon/soba in curry soup**

きつねうどん kitsune udon **udon with fried bean curd**

鍋焼きうどん nabeyaki udon **udon cooked in a clay pot with vegetables, chicken, prawn, etc.**

肉うどん/そば niku udon/soba **udon/soba in soup with sliced beef**

山菜うどん/そば sansai udon/soba **udon/soba in soup with wild vegetables**

たぬきうどん/そば tanuki udon/soba **udon/soba in soup with deep-fried light batter**

天ぷらうどん/そば tempura udon/soba **udon/soba in soup with deep-fried prawn in light batter**

天ざる tenzaru **cold soba and deep-fried prawn in light batter with dipping sauce**

ニシンそば nishin soba **soba in soup with smoked herring**

わかめうどん/そば wakame udon/soba **udon/soba in soup with seaweed**

ざるそば zaru soba **cold soba with dipping sauce**

Raamen: if you wish, add chilli powder to **miso raamen** but pepper (**koshoo**) to others.

味噌ラーメン miso raamen **raamen in soy bean paste-based soup**

塩ラーメン shio raamen **raamen in salt-based soup**

醤油ラーメン shooyu raamen **raamen in soy sauce-based soup**

チャーシュー chaashuu **raamen in soy sauce-based soup with an extra topping of sliced roast pork**

チャンポン麺 champon-men **raamen in pork stock-based soup with stir-fried meat and vegetables**

コーンラーメン koon raamen **raamen with sweet corn**

もやしラーメン moyashi raamen **raamen with extra bean sprout topping**

とんこつラーメン tonkotsu raamen **raamen in pork stock-based soup**

Rice dishes

チャーハン chaahan **Chinese style fried rice**

えび天丼 ebi-tendon **deep-fried prawn in light batter on rice**

いなり寿司 inari-zushi **seasoned rice, wrapped in fried thin bean curd**

カレーライス karee raisu **curry with rice**

おにぎり onigiri **rice ball wrapped in seaweed sheet**

親子丼 oyako-don (buri) **chicken and egg on rice**

天丼 tendon **deep-fried vegetables and prawn in light batter on rice**

うどん/そば定食 udon/soba teishoku **set meal with udon/soba, rice and side dish**

Okonomi-yaki shop

お好み焼き okonomi-yaki Japanese style pizza, sliced cabbage and meat or seafood cooked in soft dough on a hot plate

焼きそば yakisoba stir-fried Chinese noodles with meat and vegetables

焼きうどん yakiudon stir-fried thick white flour noodles with meat and vegetables

モダン焼き modan-yaki yakisoba in thin flour crêpe

広島焼き Hiroshima-yaki Hiroshima style, ingredients covered with a thin flour crêpe instead of mixing them with dough

おにぎり onigiri rice ball

You can choose what to put into **okonomi-yaki** from the following:

牛肉 gyuu-niku beef

豚肉 buta-niku pork

えび ebi shrimps

いか ika squid

たこ tako octopus

野菜 yasai vegetables (yasai-yaki is without any meat/seafood)

卵/玉子 tamago egg

In a restaurant

FACE TO FACE

…人分席を予約したいんですが
...nin bun seki o yoyaku shitain desu ga
I'd like to book a table for ... people

はい、いつですか
hai, itsu desu ka?
Yes, when for?

今夜…/明日の夜…/八時に
kon'ya.../asu no yoru.../hachi-ji ni
for tonight/for tomorrow night/at 8 o'clock

Is there a set menu?	定食はありますか teishoku wa arimasu ka?
We would like a table for ... people please	...人分のテーブルをお願いします ...nin-bun no teeburu o onegai shimasu
The menu, please	メニュー、ください menyuu, kudasai
What is the dish of the day?	今日のお薦めは何ですか kyoo no osusume wa nan desu ka?
What is the speciality of the house?	ここのお薦めは何ですか koko no osusume wa nan desu ka?
Can you tell me what this is?	これは何ですか kore wa nan desu ka?

homemade	自家製 jikasei
local delicacy	地元の珍味 jimoto no chinmi
I'll have this	これ、お願いします kore, onegai shimasu
This isn't what I ordered	これは注文したものと違います kore wa chuumon shita mono to chigaimasu
The ... is too...	この...は...過ぎます kono... wa... sugimasu

cold	冷たい	tsumetai
greasy	油っぽい	aburappoi
rare	レア	rea
salty	しょっぱい	shoppai
spicy	辛い	karai
sweet	甘い	amai
warm	温かい	atatakai
well-cooked	充分加熱された	juubun kanetsu sareta

Could we have some more ... please?	もう少し … をもらえますか moo sukoshi ... o moraemasu ka?
The bill, please	お勘定、お願いします okanjoo, onegai shimasu

Dietary requirements

coeliac	セリアック病	seriakku-byoo
dairy	乳製品	nyuuseihin
gluten	グルテン	guruten
halal	イスラム教の戒律に従った食べ物	isuramukyoo no kairitsu ni shitagatta tabemono
nuts	ナッツ	nattsu
organic	有機栽培の	yuukisaibai no
vegan	完全菜食主義	kanzen-saishokushugisha
vegetarian	ベジタリアン	bejitarian
wheat	小麦	komugi

The majority of restaurants do not indicate vegetarian food but there are always some vegetarian dishes on the menu. Don't hesitate to tell the staff that you are a vegetarian and what you can and cannot eat; they will be happy to advise you.

I have a ... allergy	...にアレルギーがあります ...ni arerugii ga arimasu
Is it ... -free?	これは...なしですか kore wa ...nashi desu ka?

I don't eat...	...は食べません ...wa tabemasen
I am a vegetarian	私はベジタリアンです watashi wa bejitarian desu
I don't eat meat	肉を食べません niku o tabemasen
I don't eat meat and fish	肉と魚を食べません niku to sakana o tabemasen
Do you have any vegetarian dishes?	野菜だけの料理はありますか yasai dake no ryoori wa arimasu ka?
Which dishes have no...?	…が入っていない料理はどれですか ...ga haitte inai ryoori wa dore desu ka?
meat	肉 niku
fish	魚 sakana
What do you recommend?	何かお薦めはありますか nanika osusume wa arimasu ka?
Is it made with vegetable or seaweed stock?	これは野菜かこぶだしで作られていますか kore wa yasai ka kobu dashi de tsukurarete imasu ka?

Possible dishes

山菜料理 sansai ryoori Japanese vegetarian dish which could be a full meal

おひたし ohitashi Japanese salad (steamed spinach or beans, etc. with sesame seeds)

味噌汁 misoshiru Japanese soup

豆腐 toofu bean curd (very popular)

冷奴 hiyayakko chilled tofu

揚げだし豆腐 agedashi doofu deep-fried tofu

卵丼 tamago domburi rice with cooked egg and vegetables (onions) in a soy sauce-based sauce

揚げだし卵 agedashi tamago Japanese omelette

巻き寿司 maki-zushi among maki-zushi, try カッパ巻き kappamaki (cucumber rolls) *or* 卵巻き tamagomaki (egg rolls)

いなり寿司 inarizushi sushi rice wrapped in fried bean curd

山菜うどん/蕎麦 sansai udon/soba udon (white Japanese flour-based noodles) *or* soba (dark coloured buckwheat noodles) in soup with vegetables

わかめうどん/蕎麦 wakame udon/soba served with seaweed

ざるそば zaru soba chilled soba with dipping sauce

野菜お好み焼き yasai okonomi-yaki Japanese style pizza with sliced cabbage, spring onion and egg, prepared on a hot plate

野菜天ぷら yasai tempura **deep-fried vegetables in a light egg batter**

きのこスパゲティー kinoko supageti **spaghetti with various Japanese mushrooms**

野菜 yasai **vegetable(s)**

山菜 sansai **edible wild plants**

Wines

If you drink at Japanese-style bars, your companions often pour drinks for each other from bottles of beer/ sake. When drinks are served, everyone raises their glasses and shouts **Kampai!** (Cheers!)

The wine list, please	ワインメニューを見せてください wain menyuu o misete kudasai
white wine	白ワイン shiro wain
red wine	赤ワイン aka wain
Can you recommend a good local sake?	地元名産のいいお酒はありますか jimoto meisan no ii osake wa arimasu ka?
house wine	ハウスワイン hausu wain

Reference

Measurements and quantities

1 lb = approx. 0.5 kilo 1 pint = approx. 0.5 litre

Liquids

1/2 litre of...	…半リットル ...han-rittoru
a litre of...	…一リットル ...ichi-rittoru
a bottle of...	…一本 ...ippon
a glass of...	…一杯 ...ippai

Weights

100 grams	百グラム hyaku-guramu
1/2 kilo of...	…五百グラム ...gohyaku-guramu

a kilo of... …一キロ
...ichi-kiro

Food

a slice of...	…一切れ ...hito-kire
a portion of...	…一山 ...hito-yama
a dozen...	…一ダース ...ichi-daasu
a box of...	…一箱 ...hito-hako
a packet of...	…一袋 ...hito-fukuro
a tin/a can of... (beer)	…一缶 ...hito-kan
a jar of...	…一瓶 ...hito-bin

Miscellaneous

...yen worth of...	…円相当の... ...en sootoo no...
a quarter	四分の一 yon-bun no ichi
20 per cent	二十パーセント nijuu-paasento

more than...	…以上 ...ijoo
less than...	…以下 ...ika
double	二倍 ni-bai
twice	二回 ni-kai

Numbers

	Chinese-derived form		Japanese form (for counting small amounts)
0	零	rei/zero	
1	一	ichi	hitotsu
2	二	ni	futatsu
3	三	san	mittsu
4	四	yon/shi	yottsu
5	五	go	itsutsu
6	六	roku	muttsu
7	七	shichi/nana	nanatsu
8	八	hachi	yattsu
9	九	kyuu/ku	kokonotsu
10	十	juu	too

Beyond ten, only the Chinese-derived form is used

11	十一	juu-ichi
12	十二	juu-ni
13	十三	juu-san
14	十四	juu-yon/shi
15	十五	juu-go
16	十六	juu-roku
17	十七	juu-shichi/nana
18	十八	juu-hachi
19	十九	juu-kyuu/ku
20	二十	nijuu
21	二十一	nijuu-ichi
22	二十二	nijuu-ni
23	二十三	nijuu-san
24	二十四	nijuu-yon/shi
25	二十五	nijuu-go
26	二十六	nijuu-roku
27	二十七	nijuu-shichi/nana
28	二十八	nijuu-hachi
29	二十九	nijuu-kyuu/ku
30	三十	san-juu
40	四十	yon-juu
50	五十	go-juu
60	六十	roku-juu
70	七十	shichi-juu/nana-juu
80	八十	hachi-juu
90	九十	kyuu-juu
100	百	hyaku
110	百十	hyaku-juu

1000	千	sen
2000	二千	ni-sen
10000	一万	ichi-man
million	百万	hyaku-man
billion	十億	juuoku

1st	一つ目 hitotsu-me	6th	六つ目 muttsu-me
2nd	二つ目 futatsu-me	7th	七つ目 nanatsu-me
3rd	三つ目 mittsu-me	8th	八つ目 yattsu-me
4th	四つ目 yottsu-me	9th	九つ目 kokonotsu-me
5th	五つ目 itsutsu-me	10th	十番目 juuban-me

Days and months

Days

Monday	月曜日	getsu-yoobi
Tuesday	火曜日	ka-yoobi
Wednesday	水曜日	sui-yoobi
Thursday	木曜日	moku-yoobi
Friday	金曜日	kin-yoobi
Saturday	土曜日	do-yoobi
Sunday	日曜日	nichi-yoobi

Months

January	一月	ichi-gatsu
February	二月	ni-gatsu
March	三月	san-gatsu
April	四月	shi-gatsu
May	五月	go-gatsu
June	六月	roku-gatsu
July	七月	shichi-gatsu
August	八月	hachi-gatsu
September	九月	ku-gatsu
October	十月	juu-gatsu
November	十一月	juuichi-gatsu
December	十二月	juuni-gatsu

Seasons

spring	春	haru
summer	夏	natsu
autumn	秋	aki
winter	冬	fuyu

What is today's date?	今日は何日ですか kyoo wa nan-nichi desu ka?
It's the 5th of March 2017	2017年の3月5日です nisen-juu-nana nen no sangatsu itsuka desu
on Saturday	土曜日に do-yoobi ni
on Saturdays/ every Saturday	毎週土曜日に maishuu do-yoobi ni
this Saturday	今週の土曜日 konshuu no do-yoobi ni
next Saturday	来週の土曜日 raishuu no do-yoobi ni
last Saturday	先週の土曜日 senshuu no do-yoobi ni
in June	6月に roku-gatsu ni
at the beginning of June	6月の初めに roku-gatsu no hajime ni

at the end of June	6月の終わりに roku-gatsu no owari ni
before summer	夏の前に natsu no mae ni
during the summer	夏の間に natsu no aida ni
after summer	夏の後に natsu no ato ni

Time

In Japan, generally the 12 hr clock is used. 24 hr clocks are used for transport timetables, but even when the timetable says 1700, people will automatically change it to 5 pm for speaking aloud.

What time is it, please?	今、何時ですか ima nan-ji desu ka?
It's...	今... ima...
am	午前 gozen
pm	午後 gogo
2 o'clock	二時です ni-ji desu

3 o'clock	三時です san-ji desu
6 o'clock	六時です roku-ji desu
It's 1 o'clock	今一時です ima ichi-ji desu
It's midday	今正午です ima shoogo desu
It's midnight	今は真夜中です ima wa mayonaka desu
9	九時 ku-ji
9.10	九時十分 ku-ji ju-ppun
quarter past 9	九時十五分 ku-ji juugo-fun
9.20	九時二十分 ku-ji niju-ppun
half past 9	九時半 ku-ji han
9.35	九時三十五分 ku-ji sanjuugo-fun
quarter to 10	十時十五分前 juu-ji juugo-fun mae
5 minutes to 10	十時五分前 juu-ji go-fun mae

Time phrases

When does it...?	いつ、...か itsu, ...ka?
open	開きます akimasu
close	閉まります shimarimasu
begin	始まります hajimarimasu
finish	終わります owarimasu
at 3 o'clock	三時に san-ji ni
before 3 o'clock	三時前に san-ji mae ni
after 3 o'clock	三時過ぎに san-ji sugi ni
today	きょう kyoo
tonight	今夜 kon'ya
tomorrow	あした ashita
yesterday	きのう kinoo

Public holidays

Most shops and offices are closed on the first three days in January. Department stores are very busy with people buying presents at the end of the year and mid-summer. Although **Obon** (13–16 August), the annual Buddhist festival to honour one's ancestors, is not a national holiday, many people take holidays and go back to their hometown so the roads and public transport become extremely busy.

Similarly, during the so-called Golden Week holiday (end of April to the beginning of May) it is extremely busy with Japanese people travelling. Make sure you have reservations in advance if you are planning to travel during these periods.

National holidays in Japan

January 1	元日 ganjitsu New Year's Day
2nd Monday in January	成人の日 seijin no hi Coming of Age Day
February 11	建国記念日 kenkoku kinen-bi National Foundation Day
Equinox Day (around March 21)	春分の日 shumbun no hi Vernal Equinox Day
April 29	昭和の日 shoowa no hi Showa Day

May 3	憲法記念日 kempoo kinen-bi Constitution Memorial Day
May 4	みどりの日 midori no hi Greenery Day
May 5	こどもの日 kodomo no hi Children's Day
3rd Monday in July	海の日 umi no hi Marine Day
August 11	山の日 yama no hi Mountain Day
3rd Monday in September	敬老の日 keiroo no hi Respect for the Aged Day
Equinox Day (around September 23)	秋分の日 shuubun no hi Autumnal Equinox Day
2nd Monday in October	体育の日 taiiku no hi Health and Sports Day
November 3	文化の日 bunka no hi National Cultural Day
November 23	勤労感謝の日 kinroo kansha no hi Labour Thanksgiving Day
December 23	天皇誕生日 tennoo tanjoobi Current Emperor's Birthday

If the national holiday falls on a Sunday, the following working day becomes the substitute holiday.

Signs and notices

Airport/station

Most signs in airports and large stations are bilingual, but local stations have little in English so the following guides will be useful.

駅	eki	station
地下鉄	chikatetsu	metro
入口	iriguchi	entrance
出口	deguchi	exit
改札口	kaisatsu guchi	ticket gate, barrier
中央改札口	chuuoo kaisatsu guchi	main gate
南口	minami guchi	south exit
西口	nishi guchi	west exit
北口	kita guchi	north exit
東口	higashi guchi	east exit
非常口	hijoo guchi	emergency exit
みどりの窓口	midori no madoguchi	JR ticket counter
切符	kippu	ticket
JRパス	jei aaru pasu	JR pass
パスポート	pasupooto	passport
引換券	hikikaeken	voucher/coupon
売り場	uriba	sales section
本日中	honjitsuchuu	today's
子供	kodomo	children

大人	otona	adult
円	en	yen
入場料	nyuujooryoo	entrance charge

Inside the station

…番線	...bansen	platform...
ホーム	hoomu	platform
エスカレーター	esukareetaa	escalator
エレベーター	erebeetaa	lift
階段	kaidan	stairs
車椅子	kurumaisu	wheelchair
昇り / 上り	nobori	going up
下り	kudari	going down

On the platform

...行き	...iki	bound for...
...発	...hatsu	depart...
...着	...chaku	arrive...
普通	futsuu	standard
急行	kyuukoo	express
特急	tokkyuu	super express
新幹線	shinkansen	bullet train
この電車	kono densha	this train
次	tsugi	next
先	saki	before
後	ato	later
通過	tsuuka	pass
停車	teisha	stop

グリーン車	guriin-sha	first class
指定席	shiteiseki	reserved
自由席	jiyuuseki	non-reserved
寝台車	shindai-sha	sleeping car
...線	...sen	line...
乗り換え	norikae	to change (buses/trains)
遅れ	okure	delay
事故	jiko	accident

Vending machines

自動販売機	jidoo-hambaiki	vending machine
水	mizu	water
お茶	ocha	Japanese tea
両替	ryoogae	money exchange
売り切れ	urikire	out of stock
故障	koshoo	out of order
つり銭切れ	tsurisengire	out of change
お釣り	otsuri	change
キオスク	kiosuku	kiosk
カード	kaado	card
押す	osu	push
引く	hiku	pull

In the carriage

開	kai	open
閉	hei	close
自動ドア・扉	jidoo doa/tobira	automatic door/ door

禁煙	kin'en	non-smoking
喫煙	kitsuen	smoking
喫煙所/喫煙室	kitsuen-jo/ -shitsu	smoking area/ room
マナーモード	manaa moodo	silent mode
食堂車	shokudoo-sha	dining car
ビュッフェ	byuffe	buffet
機内/車内販売	kinai/shanai hambai	wagon service
トイレ	toire	toilet
女	onna	women
男	otoko	men
和式	washiki	Japanese-style
洋式	yooshiki	western-style
スーツケース	suutsukeesu	suitcase

On the street (places and related words)

銀行	ginkoo	bank
薬局	yakkyoku	pharmacy
郵便局	yuubinkyoku	post office
旅館	ryokan	Japanese inn
ホテル	hoteru	hotel
ビジネスホテル	bijinesu hoteru	business hotel
レストラン	resutoran	restaurant
喫茶店	kissaten	coffee shop
モーニング サービス	mooningu saabisu	morning service (set breakfast with coffee or tea)
クリーニング	kuriiningu	dry cleaner's

スーパー	suupaa	supermarket
警察署	keisatsu-sho	police station
交番	kooban	police box
宅配	takuhai	express home delivery
空室	kuushitsu	room available
満室	manshitsu	no room/ no vacancies
開店	kaiten	shop is open
閉店	heiten	shop is closed
緊急	kinkyuu	emergency

On the street (other road signs)

危険	kiken	danger
止まれ	tomare	stop
渡れ	watare	cross
工事中	koojichuu	under construction
禁止	kinshi	prohibited
立ち入り禁止	tachiiri kinshi	no entry
右折	usetsu	right turning
左折	sasetsu	left turning
直進	chokushin	straight on
一方通行	ippoo tsuukoo	one way
歩道	hodoo	pedestrian path
自転車	jitensha	bicycle
自動車	jidoosha	automobile
歩行者	hokoosha	pedestrians

歩道橋	hodookyoo	pedestrian bridge
信号	shingoo	traffic signal

Outside the station/taxi stands

駐車場	chuushajoo	parking lot
パーキング	paakingu	parking
駐車禁止	chuusha kinshi	no parking
バス	basu	bus
タクシー	takushii	taxi
小型車	kogata-sha	small vehicle
大型車	oogata-sha	large vehicle
空車	kuu-sha	car available

At the restaurant/shop

朝食	chooshoku	breakfast
昼食	chuushoku	lunch
夕食	yuushoku	dinner
和食	washoku	Japanese meals
洋食	yooshoku	western meals
満席	manseki	full (seating)
消費税	shoohizei	consumer tax
サービス料	saabisu-ryoo	service charge
税サ込み	zeisa-komi	tax and service charge inclusive
税サ別	zeisa-betsu	tax and service charge exclusive
飲み物	nomimono	drinks

Pronouncing place names

When travelling around **Japan** (日本 nihon), you will need to bear in mind that place names as we know them are not necessarily the same as in English. Imagine if you needed to buy tickets at a train station but couldn't see your destination on the departures list, or recognise your stop being called out! This handy list eliminates such problems by indicating the pronunciations and characters for major towns and cities.

Fukuoka	福岡	fukuoka
Hiroshima	広島	hiroshima
Kobe	神戸	koobe
Kyoto	京都	kyooto
Nagasaki	長崎	nagasaki
Nagoya	名古屋	nagoya
Osaka	大阪	oosaka
Sapporo	札幌	sapporo
Tokyo	東京	tookyoo
Yokohama	横浜	yokohama

Japan's four main islands are called:

Hokkaido	北海道	hokkaidoo
Honshu	本州	honshuu
Kyushu	九州	kyuushuu
Shikoku	四国	shikoku

Grammar

Introduction

This is a guide to some of the basic concepts and rules in Japanese. It is designed to enable you to form simple sentences. There are different levels of politeness in Japanese, but polite forms, suitable for travellers to use without being rude, have been used throughout this book, including the dictionary section.

Although writing is rather complicated, Japanese grammar is fairly simple compared to that of most European languages. For example, there is no gender; there are no plural forms; and verbs only have past and non-past (present/future) forms.

Sentence structure

The basic Japanese sentence has a topic and a comment section. The topic (which is indicated by a topic marker '**wa**') usually comes at the beginning of the sentence, but if the topic is understood between the speaker and listener, it is often omitted.

(Watashi wa) Yamashita desu. (I) am Yamashita

Particles

Japanese contains particles similar to English prepositions but in Japanese they come after the relevant words. Particles have the following functions.

wa	topic marker
ga	subject marker
ka	question marker
o	direct object marker
ni	indirect object marker, goal and position marker
to	means 'and' (connecting nouns)
de	indicates means, or somewhere where an action takes place

Word order

Japanese word order is: subject – object – verb. Therefore, 'I eat sushi' becomes '**I sushi eat**'; **watashi wa sushi o tabemasu**. When the comment part is long, for example, 'I will eat sushi with my friend in London tomorrow', as long as you put **I** (which is the topic) and **will eat** (which is the verb) in their respective places and you move the object together with the necessary particle, the words can be in any order.

Questions and negatives

Polite Japanese verbs end with **masu** and sentences containing nouns and adjectives end with **desu**.

You can create a question by simply adding the question marker '**ka**' at the end of the sentence.

This is Tokyo	tokyo desu
Is it Tokyo?	tokyo desu **ka**?

Negative sentences can be made by changing the ending of the predicate such as verb or adjective accordingly.

non-past positive	non-past negative	past positive	past negative
-desu	-dewa arimasen	-deshita	-dewa arimasen deshita
-masu	-masen	-mashita	-masen deshita

I eat sushi sushi o tabe-**masu**

I don't eat sushi sushi o tabe-**masen**

I ate sushi sushi o tabe-**mashita**

I didn't eat sushi sushi o tabe-**masen deshita**

It is quiet shizuka **desu**

It is not quiet shizuka **dewa arimasen**

It was quiet shizuka **deshita**

It was not quiet shizuka **dewa arimasen deshita**

Expressing desire

Change masu to **tai desu**, for example, tabe-masu to **tabe-tai desu**, 'I would like to eat', and nomi-masu to **nomi-tai desu**, 'I would like to drink'.

Verb forms

The verbs can be divided into three groups.

The first group is verbs with stems ending in '**e**', such as tabe-masu (eat) and age-masu (give). This group also includes the verbs with one syllable (see pronunciation section) before masu such as mi-masu (watch), ki-masu (put on). A few exceptional verbs belonging to this group include: oki-masu (get up) and ori-masu (get off).

The second group is verbs with stems ending in '**i**', such as nomi-masu (drink) and kai-masu (buy).

The third group has only two verbs, shimasu and kimasu.

In order to make a request or ask permission, you need to know how to make the so-called te-form of the verbs. For the verbs in the first group, you can simply replace 'masu' with 'te': tabe-te, age-te, mi-te and ki-te. However, for the second group, you have to pay attention to which syllable comes before 'masu'.

One exception is 'ikimasu' (go): the -te form of this verb is 'itte'. And in the third group 'shimasu' is 'shite' and 'kimasu' is 'kite'.

syllable before 'masu'	change to	verb examples	te-form
shi	shite (no change)	hana**shi**-masu (talk)	hana**shite**
i, chi, ri	tte	ka**i**-masu (buy	ka**tte**
ki	ite	ki**ki**-masu (listen/ask)	ki**ite**
mi, ni, bi	nde	yo**mi**-masu (read)	yo**nde**
gi	ide	oyo**gi**-masu (swim)	oyo**ide**
ji	jite (no change)	kan**ji**-masu (feel)	kan**jite**

Making a request

If you would like someone to provide you with something, you can use the words kudasai (please give me) or onegai shimasu (please). For example, **Reshiito o kudasai**, 'Can I have a receipt please', or **Reshiito, onegai shimasu**, 'receipt please'.

If you want something to be done, use the verb te-form then add kudasai at the end: for example, 'please speak', **hanashite kudasai**; 'please buy', **katte kudasai**; 'please eat', **tabete kudasai**.

Asking permission

Use the verb te-form and add **mo ii desu ka**. Is it all right to eat? **Tabete mo ii desu ka?** Is it all right to take a photo? **Shashin o totte mo ii desu ka?** (shashin: photo(s), o: object marker, totte: te-form of verb torimasu, take).

Asking possibility/ability

Use the noun plus **dekimasu ka**. For example, 'Can we hold a meeting?' **Miitingu ga dekimasu ka?** 'Can we have a meal here?' **Koko de shokuji ga dekimasu ka?**

However, if you would like to use verbs, you must remember the three groups (see above).

For verbs in the first group, you simply change -masu to -raremasu, then add the question marker ka at the end. So, if you would like to say, 'Can we eat here?', it would be **Koko de tabe-raremasu ka?**, and 'Can we watch TV here?' would be **Koko de terebi ga mi-raremasu ka?**

For verbs in the second group, you need to change the vowel **i** in the syllable before masu to **e** as shown below.

verb examples	**change to**	**English**	**Japanese**
i**ki**-masu (go)	i**ke**-masu (can go)	Can we go to Tokyo?)	tokyoo ni ike-masu ka?
ka**i**-masu (buy)	ka**e**-masu (can buy)	Can we buy it?	sore o kae-masu ka?
ki**ki**-masu (listen/ask)	ki**ke**-masu (can listen/ask)	Can we listen to the radio?	rajio o kike-masu ka?
yo**mi**-masu (read)	yo**me**-masu (can read)	Can we read the papers?	shimbun o yome-masu ka?

For verbs in the third group, you change **shimasu** to **dekimasu** and **kimasu** to **koraremasu**.

Magic word

Sumimasen, 'excuse me' or 'sorry', is a magic word in Japanese and similar to how 'please' is used in English. As long as you use this word, especially when you are making a request, asking permission, or trying to get someone's attention, you will be fine.

English - Japanese Dictionary

*Please note that for any Japanese text with an asterisk * in the third column translation, this is the form you must use when looking up the word in a conventional dictionary (dic.).

A

a, an		see *Grammar*
abroad	海外	kaigai
accelerator	アクセル	akuseru
to accept	受理します	juri shimasu (dic. juri suru*)
do you accept credit cards?	クレジットカードでもいいですか	kurejitto kaado demo ii desu ka?
accident (traffic, etc.)	事故	jiko
accident and emergency department	救急病棟	kyuukyuu-byootoo
accommodation	宿泊所	shukuhaku-jo
account (bank)	口座	kooza
ache	痛みます	itami masu (dic. itamu*)
my head aches	頭が痛いです	atama ga itai desu
adaptor (electrical)	アダプター	adaputaa
address	住所	juusho
admission fee	入場料	nyuujooryoo
adult	大人	otona
advance: ***in advance***	前もって	maemotte
advance payment	先払い	sakibarai
advertisement	広告	kookoku

advise	アドバイスします	adobaisu shimasu (dic. adobaisu suru*)
what do you advise?	どうすればいいですか	doo sureba ii desu ka?
afford	できません	dekimasen (dic. dekiru*)
I can't afford (to buy) it	買うことができません	kau koto ga dekimasen
afternoon	午後	gogo
in the afternoon	午後に	gogo ni
this afternoon	今日の午後	kyoo no gogo
again	また	mata
age (person's)	年/歳	toshi/sai
(time)	時代	jidai
agenda (for meeting)	会議事項	kaigi jikoo
ago	前	mae
a week ago	一週間前	isshuu-kan mae
to agree (support a proposal)	賛成します	sansei shimasu (dic. sansei suru*)
I agree	賛成です	sansei desu
I don't agree	賛成しません	sansei shimasen
aid (charity)	援助	enjo
AIDS	エイズ	eizu
air	空気	kuuki
air conditioning	エアコン	eakon
air hostess	スチュワーデス	suchuwaadesu
air pollution	大気汚染	taiki-osen
airline	航空会社	kookuu-gaisha

airmail	エアメール；航空便	eameeru; kookuubin
airport	空港	kuukoo
airport bus	空港バス	kuuko-basu
alarm (in bank, shop)	警報	keihoo
alarm clock	目覚し時計	mezamashi-dokei
alcohol	(お) 酒	(o-)sake
all	全部	zembu
allergy	アレルギー	arerugii
I'm allergic to shellfish	貝類のアレルギーです	kai-rui no arerugii desu
allow	許可します	kyoka shimasu (dic. kyoka suru*)
is it allowed?	いいですか	ii desu ka?
alone	一人	hitori
always	いつも	itsumo
am (before noon)	午前	gozen
ambulance	救急車	kyuukyuu-sha
America	アメリカ	amerika
American (adj)	アメリカの	amerika no
(person)	アメリカ人	amerika-jin
anaesthetic (n)	麻酔	masui
ancestor	先祖	senzo
ancient	古代の	kodai no
and (furthermore)	そして(さらに)	soshite (sarani)
and (linking nouns)	と	to
angina	狭心症	kyooshin-shoo

angry	怒っています	okotte imasu (dic. okotte iru*)
animal	動物	doobutsu
ankle	足首	ashi-kubi
anniversary	記念日	kinembi
wedding anniversary	結婚記念日	kekkon kinembi
another (a different kind)	他の	hoka no
I'd like another	他の物が欲しいです	hoka no mono ga hoshii desu
(one more)	もう一つ	moo hitotsu
answer (written)	返事	henji
(spoken)	答え	kotae
answering machine	留守番電話	rusuban denwa
antibiotic (n)	抗生物質	koosei busshitsu
antihistamine (n)	抗ヒスタミン剤	koo-hisutamin-zai
antiseptic (n)	殺菌剤	sakkin-zai
anyone	誰でも	dare demo
anything	何でも	nan demo
anywhere	どこでも	doko demo
apartment	アパート	apaato
apologies	お詫び	owabi
my apologies (formal)	お詫びいたします	owabi itashimasu
(informal)	ごめんなさい	gomennasai
appendicitis	盲腸炎	moochoo-en
appetite	食欲	shokuyoku

apple juice	りんごジュース	ringo juusu
application (job)	申し込み	mooshikomi
appointment	約束	yakusoku
April	四月	shi-gatsu
are	あります	arimasu (dic. aru*)
are there any...?	…がありますか	...ga arimasu ka?
arm	腕	ude
to arrange	手配します	tehai shimasu (dic. tehai suru*)
can we arrange a meeting?	ミーティングを開いてもいいですか	miitingu o hiraite mo ii desu ka?
arrivals (airport)	到着	toochaku
to arrive	到着します	toochaku shimasu (dic. toochaku suru*)
art	芸術	geijutsu
art gallery	美術館	bijutsu-kan
arthritis	関節炎	kansetsu-en
artist	芸術家	geijutsu-ka
as: ***as soon as possible***	出来るだけ早く	dekiru dake hayaku
ashtray	灰皿	haizara
Asia	アジア	ajia
to ask	聞きます	kikimasu (dic. kiku*)
aspirin	アスピリン	asupirin
do you have any aspirin?	アスピリンはありますか	asupirin wa arimasu ka?
assistant (shop)	店員	ten-in
asthma	喘息	zensoku

I get asthma	喘息です	zensoku desu
at	で; に	de; ni
at home	家で	uchi de
at 4 o'clock	四時に	yo-ji ni
atmosphere (of place)	雰囲気	fun'iki
attractive	魅力的（な）	miryokuteki (na)
audience (theatre, etc.)	聴衆	chooshuu
August	八月	hachi-gatsu
aunt (own)	おば	oba
(somebody else's)	おばさん	oba-san
Australia	オーストラリア	oosutoraria
Australian (adj)	オーストラリアの	oosutoraria no
(person)	オーストラリア人	oosutoraria-jin
author	著者	chosha
automatic (door)	自動 (ドア)	jidoo (doa)
autumn	秋	aki
available	手に入ります	te ni hairimasu (dic. te ni hairu*)
when will it be available?	いつ頃手手に入りますか	itsu goro te ni hairimasu ka?
avalanche	雪崩れ	nadare
away	留守	rusu
I will be away in August	八月は留守です	hachi-gatsu wa rusu desu

B

baby	赤ちゃん	aka-chan
baby food	離乳食	rinyuu-shoku
baby seat	ベビーシート	bebii shiito
back (of body)	背中	senaka
(v) (be back)	戻ります	modorimasu (dic. modoru*)
when will he be back?	いつ戻りますか	itsu modorimasu ka?
bad (character, morally)	悪い	warui
(food)	腐った	kusatta
bag	鞄	kaban
baggage	荷物	nimotsu
baggage reclaim	手荷物受取所	tenimotsu uketori-sho
baker's	パン屋	pan-ya
ball	ボール	booru
bandage	包帯	hootai
bank	銀行	ginkoo
bar (to drink in)	バー; 居酒屋	baa; izakaya
barber's	床屋	toko-ya
bargain	バーゲン	baagen
baseball	野球	yakyuu
basement	地下	chika
basket	かご	kago
basketball	バスケットボール	basukettobooru
bath	風呂	furo
bathroom	浴室	yokushitsu

bath towel	バスタオル	basu taoru
bath (tub)	浴槽	yokusoo
battery (for radio, etc.)	電池	denchi
(for car)	バッテリー	batterii
beach	浜辺	hamabe
bean	豆	mame
bean curd	豆腐	toofu
beautiful	きれい（な）	kirei (na)
bed (western)	ベッド	beddo
(Japanese)	布団	futon
double bed	ダブルベッド	daburu beddo
single bed	シングルベッド	shinguru beddo
bedding	寝具	shingu
bedroom	寝室	shinshitsu
beef	牛肉	gyuu-niku
beer	ビール	biiru
draught beer	生ビール	nama biiru
before	前(に)	mae (ni)
before 4 o'clock	四時前に	yo-ji mae ni
before next week	今週中に	konshuu chuu ni
to begin	始まります	hajimarimasu (dic. hajimaru*)
to begin (something)	始めます	hajimemasu (dic. hajimeru*)
to belong to	属します	zokushimasu (dic. zokusuru*)
it/they belong(s) to me	私のです	watashi no desu

B

English - Japanese

does this belong to you?	あなたのですか	anata no desu ka?
belt	ベルト	beruto
beside	隣	tonari
can I sit beside you?	隣に座ってもいいですか	tonari ni suwatte mo ii desu ka?
best	一番	ichiban
I like this the best	これが一番好きです	kore ga ichiban suki desu
bicycle	自転車	jitensha
big	大きい	ookii
bigger	もっと大きい	motto ookii
have you anything bigger?	もっと大きいのはありませんか	motto ookii no wa arimasen ka?
bike	自転車	jitensha
mountain bike	マウンテンバイク	maunten baiku
bill	(お) 勘定	(o-) kanjoo
binoculars	望遠鏡	booenkyoo
bird	鳥	tori
birthday	誕生日	tanjoobi
happy birthday!	誕生日おめでとう	tanjoobi omedetoo!
birthday present	誕生日プレゼント	tanjoobi purezento
biscuits	ビスケット	bisuketto
bit	少し	sukoshi
just a bit	ほんの少し	hon no sukoshi
to bite	噛みます	kamimasu (dic. kamu*)
bitter (taste)	苦い	nigai
black (n)	黒	kuro

(adj)	黒い; 黒の	kuroi; kuro no
blanket	毛布	moofu
to bleed	血が出ます	chi ga demasu (dic. chi ga deru*)
it won't stop bleeding	血が止まりません	chi ga tomarimasen
blind (person)	目の不自由（な）	me no fujiyuu (na)
(for window)	ブラインド	buraindo
blocked	詰まった	tsumatta
the sink is blocked	流しが詰まっています	nagashi ga tsumatte imasu
blood	血; 血液	chi; ketsueki
blood group	血液型	ketsueki-gata
my blood group is B	(私の) 血液型はBです	(watashi no) ketsueki-gata wa 'B' desu
blood pressure	血圧	ketsuatsu
I have high blood pressure	私は高血圧です	watashi wa koo-ketsuatsu desu
blue (n)	青	ao
(adj)	青い	aoi
to board (plane, train)	乗ります	norimasu (dic. noru*)
boarding pass	搭乗券	toojoo-ken
boat	ボート	booto
boiled rice	ご飯	gohan
bone	骨	hone
bonito	鰹	katsuo
book (reading)	本	hon

to book	予約します	yoyaku shimasu (dic. yoyaku suru*)
booking	予約	yoyaku
boots	ブーツ	buutsu
born	生まれます	umaremasu (dic. umareru*)
I was born in Scotland	(私は) スコットランドで生まれました	(watashi wa) Sukottorando de umaremashita
to borrow	借ります	karimasu (dic. kariru*)
can I borrow...?	…を借りてもいいですか	...o karite mo ii desu ka?
botanical gardens	植物園	shokubutsu-en
bottle	瓶; ボトル	bin; botoru
bottle opener	栓抜き	sennuki
bowl	ボール; 椀	booru; wan
box	箱	hako
boy	男の子	otokonoko
boyfriend	彼; 彼氏	kare; kareshi
bra	ブラ	bura
brakes	ブレーキ	bureeki
branch (bank)	支店	shiten
(company)	支社	shisha
(of tree)	枝	eda
brandy	ブランデー	burandee
bread	パン	pan
to break	壊します	kowashimasu (dic. kowasu*)
It has broken down	故障しました	koshoo shimashita

breakfast	朝食; 朝ご飯	chooshoku; asa-gohan
breast (chicken)	(鶏の) 胸肉	(tori no) mune-niku
to breathe	息をします	iki o shimasu (dic. iki o suru*)
I can't breathe	息ができません	iki ga dekimasen
bride	新婦	shimpu
bridegroom	新郎	shinroo
bridge (game)	ブリッジ	burijji
(over river, road, etc.)	橋	hashi
briefcase	ブリーフケース	buriifukeesu
to bring (thing)	持って来ます	motte kimasu (dic. motte kuru*)
(person)	連れて来ます	tsurete kimasu (dic. tsurete kuru*)
Britain	イギリス; 英国	Igirisu; Eikoku
British (adj)	イギリスの	Igirisu no
(person)	イギリス人	Igirisu-jin
brochure	パンフレット	panfuretto
brothers	兄弟	kyoodai
brother (own, younger)	弟	otooto
(own, older)	兄	ani
(somebody else's, younger)	弟さん	otooto-san
(somebody else's, older)	お兄さん	onii-san
brown (n)	茶色	chairo
(adj)	茶色い	chairoi
Buddha	仏	hotoke

Buddhism	仏教	bukkyoo
Buddhist temple	(お) 寺	(o-) tera
building	建物; ビル	tatemono; biru
bulb (light)	電球	denkyuu
bullet train	新幹線	shinkansen
bureau de change	両替所	ryoogae-jo
burn	こがします	kogashimasu (dic. kogasu*)
It's burnt (food)	こげています	kogete imasu
bus	バス	basu
by bus	バスで	basu de
business	ビジネス; 仕事	bijinesu; shigoto
business card	名刺	meishi
business trip	出張	shutchoo
bus stop	バス停	basutei
bus tour	バスツアー	basu tsuaa
is there a bus tour?	バスツアーがありますか	basu tsuaa ga arimasu ka?
busy	忙しい	isogashii
are you busy?	忙しいですか	isogashii desu ka?
the line is busy (phone)	話し中です	hanashi-chuu desu
butcher's	肉屋	niku-ya
butter	バター	bataa
button	ボタン	botan
to buy	買います	kaimasu (dic. kau*)
where can I buy...?	どこで買えますか	doko de kaemasu ka?

C

cable car	ロープウェイ	roopuwei
caddy (golf)	キャディー	kyadii
café	喫茶店	kissaten
cake (western-style)	ケーキ	keeki
cake shop	ケーキ屋	keeki-ya
calculator	計算機	keisanki
to call (phone)	…に電話をかけます	...ni denwa o kakemasu (dic. denwa o kakeru*)
long-distance call	長距離電話	chookyori denwa
camcorder	ビデオカメラ	bideo kamera
camera	カメラ	kamera
camera shop	カメラ屋	kamera-ya
camping	キャンプ	kyampu
can (n)	缶	kan
can (v)	出来ます	dekimasu (dic. dekiru*)
can I...?	…出来ますか	...dekimasu ka?
Canada	カナダ	Kanada
Canadian (adj)	カナダの	Kanada no
(person)	カナダ人	Kanada-jin
to cancel	取り消します	torikeshimasu (dic. torikesu*)
I'd like to cancel my booking	予約を取り消したいです	yoyaku o torikeshitai desu
cancellation (of flight)	欠航	kekkoo
(of train)	運休	unkyuu
cancer	癌	gan

canned	缶詰	kanzume
can opener	缶切	kankiri
capital (city)	首都	shuto
(money)	資金	shikin
car	車; 自動車	kuruma; jidoosha
caravan	キャラバン	kyaraban
card (business)	名刺	meishi
(playing)	トランプ	torampu
(greetings)	カード	kaado
cardphone	カード用電話	kaado-yoo denwa
careful	気をつけます	ki o tsukemasu (dic. ki o tsukeru*)
be careful!	気をつけて	ki o tsukete!
careless	不注意	fuchuui
car keys	車の鍵	kuruma no kagi
car park	駐車場	chuushajoo
carpet	絨毯; カーペット	juutan; kaapetto
carriage (train)	客車	kyakusha
carrier bag	買い物袋	kaimono bukuro
carrot	人参	ninjin
to carry	運びます	hakobimasu (dic. hakobu*)
carsick	車酔い	kurumayoi
I get carsick	車に酔います	kuruma ni yoimasu (dic. kuruma ni you*)
carwash	洗車	sensha
case (suitcase)	スーツケース; 旅行鞄	suutsukeesu; ryokoo kaban
cash (n)	現金	genkin

English	Japanese	Romanization
we only take cash	現金払いのみです	genkin barai nomi desu
casino	カジノ	kajino
castle	お城	shiro
cat	猫	neko
to catch (hold of)	つかみます	tsukamimasu (dic. tsukamu*)
to catch a cold	風邪をひきます	kaze o hikimasu (dic. kaze o hiku*)
cathedral	大聖堂	daiseidoo
Catholic	カトリック	katorikku
cauliflower	カリフラワー	karifurawaa
cave	洞窟	dookutsu
CD	シーディー	shiidii
CD player	シーディープレーヤー	shiidii pureiyaa
cell phone	携帯電話	keitai denwa
cemetery	墓地	bochi
centigrade	摂氏	sesshi
centimetre	センチ(メートル)	senchi (meetoru)
central	中心の	chuushin no
central heating	セントラルヒーティング	sentoraru hiitingu
centre	中心; 中央	chuushin; chuuoo
century	世紀	seiki
21st century	二十一世紀	nijuu-isseiki
ceramics	陶器	tooki
certain	確か（な）	tashika (na)
are you certain?	本当ですか	hontoo desu ka?
certainly (truth)	確かに	tashika (na)

certainly! (I will do that)	喜んで	yorokonde!
chair	椅子	isu
champagne	シャンペン	shampen
change (money)	小銭	kozeni
changing room	更衣室	kooi-shitsu
charge (fee)	手数料	tesuuryoo
is there any charge?	手数料はかかりますか	tesuuryoo wa kakarimasu ka?
free of charge	無料	muryoo
to check	調べます; チェックします	shirabemasu (dic. shiraberu*); chekku shimasu (dic. chekku suru*)
can you check this for me?	これを調べてください	kore o shirabete kudasai?
to check in	チェックインします	chekku-in shimasu (dic. chekku-in suru*)
where do I check in?	チェックインはどこでしますか	chekku-in wa doko de shimasuka?
check-in desk (hotel)	フロント	furonto
to check out	チェックアウトします	chekku-auto shimasu (dic. chekku-auto suru*)
when should I check out by?	チェックアウトは何時ですか	chekku-auto wa nan-ji desu ka?
cheese	チーズ	chiizu
chef	シェフ	shefu
chemist's (shop)	薬屋; 薬局	kusuriya; yakkyoku

cherry blossom	桜	sakura
chest (of body)	胸	mune
chewing gum	チューインガム	chuuin-gamu
chicken (bird)	鶏	niwatori
(meat)	鶏肉	toriniku
(grilled)	焼き鳥	yaki-tori
chickenpox	水ぼうそう	mizuboosoo
child	子供	kodomo
children	子供達	kodomo-tachi
chilli	唐辛子	toogarashi
china (n)	瀬戸物	setomono
China	中国	Chuugoku
Chinese (adj)	中国の	Chuugoku no
(person)	中国人	Chuugoku-jin
(language)	中国語	Chuugoku-go
chips (french fries)	フライドポテト	furaido poteto
chocolate(s)	チョコレート	chokoreeto
to choose	選びます	erabimasu (dic. erabu*)
I don't know what to choose	どれにしたらいいかわかりません	dore ni shitara ii ka wakarimasen
you choose for me	代わりに選んでください	kawari ni erande kudasai
chopsticks	(お) 箸	(o-)hashi
Christmas	クリスマス	kurisumasu
Christmas Eve	クリスマスイブ	kurisumasu-ibu
church	教会	kyookai
cigar	葉巻	hamaki

cigarette	煙草	tabako
cigarette lighter	ライター	raitaa
cinema	映画館	eiga-kan
city	町; 都会	machi; tokai
city centre	町の中心	machi no chuushin
claim (n)	要求	yookyuu
class (in school)	組; クラス	kumi; kurasu
business class	ビジネスクラス	bijinesu kurasu
economy class	エコノミークラス	ekonomii kurasu
first class	ファーストクラス	faasuto kurasu
classical music	クラシック	kurashikku
clean (adj)	きれい（な）	kirei (na)
to clean (house)	掃除します	sooji shimasu (dic. sooji suru*)
cleaner (company)	清掃業者	seisoo gyoosha
clever	賢い	kashikoi
climate	気候; 風土	kikoo; fuudo
climbing (mountains)	山登り	yama nobori
climbing boots	登山靴	tozan gutsu
clinic	クリニック; 診療所	kurinikku; shinryoo-jo
clock	時計	tokei
to close	閉めます	shimemasu (dic. shimeru*)
when do you close?	いつ閉まりますか	itsu shimarimasu ka?
closed (shops)	閉店	heiten
clothes	服	fuku
cloudy	曇っている	kumotte iru

club	クラブ	kurabu
clutch (car)	クラッチ	kuratchi
coach (bus)	バス	basu
(of train)	客車	kyakusha
coach station	バス乗り場	basu noriba
coast	海岸	kaigan
coat	コート; 上着	kooto; uwagi
Coca Cola®	コカコーラ	kokakoora
coffee	コーヒー	koohii
black coffee	ブラックコーヒー	burakku koohii
white coffee	ミルクコーヒー	miruku koohii
decaffeinated coffee	カフェイン抜きのコーヒー	kafein nuki no koohii
cappuccino	カプチーノ	kapuchiino
cognac	コニャック	konyakku
coin	コイン; …玉	koin; -dama
ten-yen coin	十円玉	juu-en-dama
cold (room)	寒い	samui
(illness)	風邪	kaze
I have a cold	風邪をひいています	kaze o hiite imasu
colleague	同僚	dooryoo
college (university)	大学	daigaku
(junior college)	短大	tandai
colour	色	iro
comb	くし	kushi
to come	来ます	kimasu (dic. kuru*)

when can you come?	いつ来られますか	itsu koraremasu ka?
come in!	どうぞお入りください	doozo ohairi kudasai!
comedy	コメディー	komedii
comfortable	気持ちがいい	kimochi ga ii
this is very comfortable	これはとても気持ちがいいです	kore wa totemo kimochi ga ii desu
comics (publications)	漫画	manga
commercial (on TV)	コマーシャル	komaasharu
common (usual)	普通の	futsuu (no)
compact disc	コンパクトディスク; CD	kompakuto disuku; shii dii
company (firm)	会社	kaisha
company president	社長; 常務	shachoo; joomu
compartment (train)	車両	sharyoo
complaint	苦情	kujoo
I have a complaint	苦情があります	kujoo ga arimasu
to complete	完成します	kansei shimasu (dic. kansei suru*)
complicated	複雑（な）	fukuzatsu (na)
it's very complicated	とても複雑です	totemo fukuzatsu desu
compulsory	義務	gimu
computer	コンピューター	kompyuutaa
computer game	コンピューターゲーム	kompyuutaa geemu

concert	コンサート	konsaato
concert hall	コンサートホール	konsaato hooru
concussion (brain)	脳震盪	nooshintoo
conditioner (hair)	リンス	rinsu
condom	コンドーム	kondoomu
conductor (music)	指揮者	shikisha
conference	会議	kaigi
conference centre	会議場	kaigijoo
to confirm	確認します	kakunin shimasu (dic. kakunin suru*)
do I need to confirm?	確認する必要がありますか	kakunin suru hitsuyoo ga arimasu ka?
I want to confirm my booking	予約の確認をお願いします	yoyaku no kakunin o onegai shimasu
congratulations	おめでとうございます	omedetoo gozaimasu
to connect	つなぎます	tsunagimasu (dic. tsunagu*)
I'm trying to connect you	おつなぎしています	otsunagi shite imasu
connection (train, plane)	乗り継ぎ	noritsugi
(electronic)	接続	setsuzoku
constipated	便秘	bempi
I'm constipated	便秘です	bempi desu
consul	領事	ryooji
consulate	領事館	ryoojikan
contact lens cleaner	コンタクトレンズ洗浄液	kontakuto renzu senjooeki

C

English - Japanese

contact lenses	コンタクトレンズ	kontakuto renzu
continent	大陸	tairiku
contraceptive (n)	避妊薬; 避妊用品	hinin-yaku; hinin-yoohin
convenient	便利（な）; 都合のいい	benri (na); tsugoo no ii
cook (n)	コック	kokku
(Japanese restaurants)	板前	itamae
to cook	料理します	ryoori shimasu (dic. ryoori suru*)
copy (n)	コピー	kopii
can I make a copy?	コピーをしてもいいですか	kopii o shite mo ii desu ka?
corkscrew	栓抜き	sen-nuki
corn	とうもろこし	toomorokoshi
corner	角	kado
correct	正しい	tadashii
is it correct?	正しいですか	tadashii desu ka?
corridor	廊下	rooka
cost (n)	費用; コスト	hiyoo; kosuto
to cost	かかります	kakarimasu (dic. kakaru*)
how much does it cost?	いくらかかりますか	ikura kakarimasu ka?
cotton	綿	wata/men
cough (n)	咳	seki
to count	数えます	kazoemasu (dic. kazoeru*)
country	国	kuni

countryside	田舎	inaka
courier	宅配	takuhai
course	コース	koosu
of course	勿論	mochiron
court (law)	法廷	hootei
(tennis)	テニスコート	tenisu kooto
crab	カニ	kani
crafts	工芸品	koogei hin
cramp	けいれん; こむらがえり	keiren; komuragaeri
crayfish	ザリガニ	zarigani
cream	クリーム	kuriimu
credit	信用	shin'yoo
credit card	クレジットカード	kurejitto kaado
crisps	ポテトチップス	poteto chippusu
crossing (ferry)	フェリー	ferii
when is the next crossing?	次のフェリーは何時ですか	tsugi no ferii wa nan-ji desu ka?
crossroads	十字路	juujiro
crowd	人ごみ	hitogomi
cruise (n)	船旅	funatabi
to cry (weep)	泣きます	nakimasu (dic. naku*)
cup	カップ	kappu
cupboard	戸棚	todana
to cure	治療します	chiryoo shimasu (dic. chiryoosuru*)
current (electricity)	電流	denryuu
curtains	カーテン	kaaten

cushion	クッション	kusshion
customs	税関	zeikan
customs declaration	税関申告	zeikan shinkoku
cut (n)	切り傷	kirikizu
to cut	切ります	kirimasu (dic. kiru*)
cybercafé	インターネットカフェ	intaanetto kafe
cycling	サイクリング	saikuringu

D

daily (each day)	毎日の	mainichi (no)
dance	踊り; ダンス	odori; dansu
to dance	踊ります	odorimasu (*dic. odoru)
dangerous	危ない; 危険	abunai; kiken
dark	暗い	kurai
date (day of month)	日付	hizuke
date of birth	生年月日	seinen-gappi
daughter (own)	娘	musume
(somebody else's)	娘さん; お嬢さん	musume-san; o-joo-san
day	日	nichi
per day	一日に	ichi-nichi ni
every day	毎日	mai-nichi
deaf	耳の聞こえない	mimi no kikoenai
dear (expensive)	高い; 高価	takai; kooka
decaffeinated	カフェイン抜きの	kafein nuki (no)

December	十二月	juuni-gatsu
deep	深い	fukai
degree (temperature)	度	do
(university)	学位	gakui
delay	遅れ	okure
how long is the delay?	どのぐらい遅れますか	donogurai okuremasu ka?
to be delayed (plane, train, etc.)	遅れます	okuremasu (dic. okureru*)
dentist	歯医者	ha-isha
dentures	義歯; 入れ歯	gishi; ireba
department store	デパート	depaato
departure	出発	shuppatsu
departure lounge	出発ラウンジ	shuppatsu raunji
deposit (to pay)	保証金	hoshookin
dessert	デザート	dezaato
destination	目的地	mokutekichi
detergent	洗剤	senzai
diabetes	糖尿病	toonyoobyoo
to dial	ダイヤルします	daiyaru shimasu (dic. daiyaru suru*)
dialling code	局番	kyokuban
diarrhoea	下痢	geri
diary (journal)	日記	nikki
dictionary	辞書	jisho
different	違う	chigau
digital camera	デジタルカメラ	dejitaru kamera

dining room	ダイニングルーム; 食堂	dainingu-ruumu; shokudoo
dinner	夕食; 晩ごはん	yuushoku; ban-gohan
direct (train, etc.)	直通	chokutsuu
direction	方向	hookoo
directory (telephone)	電話帳	denwa-choo
dirty	汚い	kitanai
disabled	障害のある	shoogai no aru
disco	ディスコ	disuko
discount	割引	waribiki
dish	(お) 皿	(o-)sara
disinfectant	消毒薬	shoodoku-yaku
disk	ディスク	disuku
disposable	使い捨ての	tsukaisute no
district	地方	chihoo
divorce (n)	離婚	rikon
divorced	離婚した	rikon shita
dizzy	めまい	memai
to feel dizzy	めまいがします	memai ga shimasu (dic. memai ga suru*)
to do	します	shimasu (dic. suru*)
doctor	医者	isha
document	文書	bunsho
dog	犬	inu
dollar	ドル	doru
door	戸; ドア	to; doa
double	二重の	nijuu no
(quantity)	二倍の	nibai no

double bed	ダブルベッド	daburu beddo
double room	ダブルルーム; 二人部屋	daburu ruumu; futari beya
download	ダウンロードします	daunroodo shimasu (dic. daunroodo suru*)
dress (n) (everyday)	ワンピース	wanpiisu
(formal)	ドレス	doresu
dressing (medical)	包帯	hootai
(salad)	ドレッシング	doresshingu
drink	飲み物	nomimono
to drink	飲みます	nomimasu (dic. nomu*)
to drive	運転します; ドライブします	unten shimasu (dic. unten suru); doraibu shimasu (dic. doraibu suru*)
driver (of car)	運転手	untenshu
driving licence	運転免許証	unten-menkyoshoo
drug (medical)	薬; 薬品	kusuri; yakuhin
to dry (clothes, etc.)	乾かします	kawakashimasu (dic. kawakasu*)
dry-cleaner's	ドライクリーニング	dorai-kuriiningu
duck	アヒル	ahiru
duty-free	免税の	menzei (no)
duvet	掛け布団	kakebuton

E

ear	耳	mimi
earache	耳が痛い	mimi ga itai

early	早く	hayaku
earplugs	耳栓	mimi-sen
earrings	イヤリング	iyaringu
earthquake	地震	jishin
east	東	higashi
Easter	イースター	iisutaa
to eat	食べます	tabemasu (dic. taberu*)
eel	うなぎ	unagi
egg	卵; 玉子	tamago
fried egg	目玉焼き	medama-yaki
hard-boiled egg	硬ゆで卵	kata yude tamago
scrambled eggs	炒り玉子	iri tamago
elastic	輪ゴム	wa-gomu
electrician	電気屋	denki-ya
electricity	電気	denki
electric razor	電気かみそり	denki-kamisori
elevator	エレベーター	erebeetaa
e-mail	電子メール; メール	denshi-meeru; meeru
embassy	大使館	taishikan
emergency	緊急	kinkyuu
emergency exit	非常口	hijoo-guchi
emperor	天皇	tennoo
empty	空	kara
engaged (couple)	婚約している	kon'yaku shite iru
(phone)	話し中	hanashi-chuu
(toilet)	使用中	shiyoo-chuu
England	イングランド	ingurando

English (adj)	イングランドの	ingurando no
(person)	イングランド人	ingurando-jin
(language)	英語	eigo
enough	十分	juubun
that's enough (food, etc.)	もう結構です	moo kekkoo desu
enquiry desk	受付	uketsuke
to enter (a place)	入ります	hairimasu (dic. hairu*)
entrance	入口	iriguchi
entrance fee	入場料	nyuujooryoo
envelope	封筒	fuutoo
equipment	設備	setsubi
escalator	エスカレーター	esukareetaa
euro	ユーロ	yuuro
Europe	ヨーロッパ	yooroppa
evening	夜; 晩	yoru; ban
in the evening	夜に	yoru ni
evening meal	夕食; 晩ごはん	yuushoku; ban-gohan
example	例	rei
for example	たとえば	tatoeba
excellent	素晴らしい	subarashii
excess baggage	超過手荷物	chooka tenimotsu
exchange rate	為替レート	kawase reeto
excursion	遠出	toode
excuse me	すみません	sumimasen
exhibition	展示会	tenjikai
exit	出口	deguchi
expensive	高い; 高価(な)	takai; kooka (na)

exports	輸出品	yushutsu-hin
express train	急行	kyuukoo
extension (electrical)	延長コード	enchoo koodo
(phone)	内線	naisen
eye	目	me
eye drops	目薬	megusuri

F

fabric	生地	kiji
factory	工場	koojoo
to faint	気絶します	kizetsu shimasu (dic. kizetsu suru*)
false teeth	入れ歯	ireba
family	家族	kazoku
fan (hand-held)	うちわ; 扇子	uchiwa; sensu
(electric)	扇風機	sempuuki
far	遠い	tooi
fare (bus, etc.)	料金	ryookin
Far East	極東	kyokutoo
farm	農家	nooka
fast	速い	hayai
fat (person)	太った	futotta
father (own)	父	chichi
(somebody else's)	お父さん	otoo-san
faulty (machine, etc.)	欠陥のある	kekkan no aru
fax	ファックス	fakkusu
fax number	ファックス番号	fakkusu bangoo

to fax	ファックスを送ります	fakkusu o okurimasu (dic. fakkusu o okuru*)
February	二月	ni-gatsu
fee	料金	ryookin
female (adj)	女の	onna no
ferry	フェリー	ferii
festival	祭り	matsuri
few	少ない	sukunai
a few	二、三の	ni, san no
fiancé(e)	フィアンセ; 婚約者	fianse; kon'yaku-sha
file (computer, document)	ファイル	fairu
filling (tooth)	詰め物	tsumemono
film (cinema)	映画	eiga
to find	見つけます	mitsukemasu (dic. mitsukeru*)
I can't find...	…が見つかりません	...ga mitsukarimasen
fine (penalty)	罰金	bakkin
finger	指	yubi
fire	火	hi
house fire	家事; 火災	kaji; kasai
camp fire	焚き火	takibi
fire alarm	火災報知器	kasai-hoochi-ki
fire brigade	消防隊	shooboo-tai
fire escape	非常階段	hijoo-kaidan
fire extinguisher	消火器	shookaki
fireworks	花火	hanabi

firm (company)	会社	kaisha
first	最初の	saisho (no)
first aid	応急手当	ookyuu-teate
first aid kit	救急箱	kyuukyuu-bako
first class	ファーストクラス	faasuto kurasu
first name	名前	namae
fish (n)	魚	sakana
to fit	合います	aimasu (dic. au*)
it doesn't fit	合いません	aimasen
fitting room	試着室	shichaku-shitsu
to fix	直します	naoshimasu (dic. naosu*)
can you fix it?	直せますか	naosemasu ka?
flat (apartment)	アパート	apaato
(battery)	バッテリーがあがります	batterii ga agarimasu (dic. batterii ga agaru*)
flat tyre	パンク	panku
flavour	味	aji
floor (of building)	…階	...kai
(of room)	床	yuka
ground floor	一階	ikkai
first floor	二階	ni-kai
second floor	三階	san-gai
flower	花	hana
flu	インフルエンザ	infuruenza
fly (insect)	ハエ	hae
to fly	飛びます	tobimasu (dic.tobu*)

food	食べ物	tabemono
food poisoning	食中毒	shokuchuu-doku
foot	足	ashi
football (soccer)	サッカー	sakkaa
for (in exchange for)	…の代わりに	...no kawari ni
foreign	外国の	gaikoku no
forest	森	mori
fork (cutlery)	フォーク	fooku
fortnight	二週間	ni-shuu-kan
fountain	泉; 噴水	izumi; funsui
foyer	ロビー	robii
fracture (of bone)	骨折	kossetsu
fragrance	香り	kaori
frame (picture)	額	gaku
free (not occupied)	空いています	aite imasu (dic. aite iru*)
(costing nothing)	無料の	muryoo (no)
(not constrained)	自由 (な)	jiyuu (na)
fresh (food)	新鮮 (な)	shinsen (na)
Friday	金曜日	kin-yoobi
fridge	冷蔵庫	reizooko
fried food	揚げ物	agemono
friend	友だち	tomodachi
fruit	果物	kudamono
fruit juice	フルーツジュース	furuutsu juusu
fuel	燃料	nenryoo
full	いっぱい	ippai

full board	三食付の宿泊	san-shoku tsuki no shukuhaku
funny (amusing)	面白い	omoshiroi
(strange)	おかしい; かわった	okashii; kawatta
fuse	ヒューズ	hyuuzu
fuse box	ヒューズボックス	hyuuzu bokkusu

G

gallery	ギャラリー; 画廊	gyararii; garoo
game	ゲーム	geemu
garage	ガレージ; 車庫	gareeji; shako
garden	庭	niwa
garlic	にんにく	ninniku
gastritis	胃炎	ien
gate	門	mon
(airport)	ゲート; 搭乗口	geeto; toojoo guchi
gay (bright)	華やか（な）	hanayaka (na)
(homosexual)	ゲイ	gei
gears	ギア	gia
(cogs)	歯車	haguruma
generous	寛大（な）	kandai (na)
gentleman	紳士	shinshi
gents (toilet)	男性用トイレ	dansei-yoo toire
to get (obtain)	手に入れます	te ni iremasu (dic. te ni ireru*)
(to fetch something)	持ってきます	motte kimasu (dic. motte kuru*)

(to fetch person, animal)	連れてきます	tsurete kimasu (dic. tsurete kuru*)
to get in (car)	乗ります	norimasu (dic. noru*)
to get off (bus, etc.)	降ります	orimasu (dic. oriru*)
gift	贈り物; プレゼント	okurimono; purezento
gift shop	ギフトショップ	gifuto shoppu
ginger	しょうが	shooga
girl (informal)	少女; 女の子	shoojo; onnanoko
(polite)	お嬢さん	ojoo-san
girlfriend	彼女	kanojo
to give	あげます	agemasu (dic. ageru*)
to give back	返します	kaeshimasu (dic. kaesu*)
glass	グラス; コップ	gurasu; koppu
glasses (spectacles)	めがね	megane
gloves	手袋	tebukuro
glue	のり	nori
to go	行きます	ikimasu (dic. iku*)
to go back	戻ります	modorimasu (dic. modoru*)
to go in	入ります	hairimasu (dic. hairu*)
gold	金	kin
golf	ゴルフ	gorufu
golf ball	ゴルフボール	gorufu booru
golf club	ゴルフクラブ	gorufu kurabu
golf course	ゴルフコース	gorufu koosu
good	よい; いい	yoi; ii
good afternoon	こんにちは	konnichiwa

G

goodbye	さようなら	sayoonara
good evening	こんばんは	kombanwa
good morning	おはようございます	ohayoo gozaimasu
good night	おやすみなさい	oyasuminasai
to go out	出かけます	dekakemasu (dic. dekakeru*)
granddaughter	孫娘	mago-musume
grandfather (own)	祖父	sofu
(somebody else's)	おじいさん	ojii-san
grandmother (own)	祖母	sobo
(somebody else's)	おばあさん	obaa-san
grandson	孫息子	mago-musuko
grapefruit	グレープフルーツ	gureepufuruutsu
grapes	ぶどう	budoo
great (large)	大きい	ookii
green (n)	緑	midori
(adj)	緑の	midori no
greengrocer	八百屋	yao-ya
grey (n)	灰色; グレー	haiiro; guree
(adj)	灰色の; グレーの	haiiro-no; guree-no
grilled	焼いた; 焼き…	yaita; yaki...
grocer's	食料品店	shokuryoohin-ten
ground floor	一階	ikkai
group (people)	グループ; 組	guruupu; kumi
guarantee (n)	保証	hoshoo
guest (to house)	お客様	okyaku-sama
guest house	ゲストハウス	gesuto hausu

guide (n)	ガイド; 案内	gaido; annai
to guide	案内をします	annai o shimasu (dic. annai o suru*)
guidebook	ガイドブック	gaido bukku
guided tour	ガイドツアー	gaido tsuaa

H

hair	髪; 髪の毛	kami; kaminoke
hairbrush	ブラシ	burashi
haircut (for men)	散髪	sampatsu
(for women)	ヘアーカット	heaakatto
hairdresser's (for men)	床屋	tokoya)
(for women)	美容院	biyooin
hair dryer	ヘアードライヤー	heaa doraiyaa
half-price	半額	hangaku
hall (for concerts, etc.)	ホール	hooru
ham	ハム	hamu
handbag	ハンドバッグ	handobaggu
handicapped (person)	身体障害者	shintai shoogaisha
handkerchief	ハンカチ	hankachi
hand luggage	手荷物	tenimotsu
hand-made	手作りの	tezukuri-no
to happen	起こります	okorimasu (dic. okoru*)
what happened?	どうしましたか	doo shimashita ka?

hard (firm)	かたい	katai
(difficult)	難しい	muzukashii
hay fever	花粉症	kafunshoo
head	頭	atama
headache	頭痛	zutsuu
headlights	ヘッドライト	heddoraito
head office	本社	honsha
headphones	ヘッドホン	heddohon
hearing aid	補聴器	hochooki
heart (emotional)	心	kokoro
(organ)	心臓	shinzoo
heart attack	心臓発作	shinzoo hossa
to heat up (food)	温めます	atatamemasu (dic. atatameru*)
heater	ヒーター	hiitaa
heavy (weight)	重い	omoi
hello	こんにちは	konnichiwa
(on phone)	もしもし	moshi moshi
to help	手伝います	tetsudaimasu (dic. tetsudau*)
help!	助けて	tasukete!
here	ここ	koko
high	高い	takai
high blood pressure	高血圧	koo-ketsuatsu
hill-walking	ハイキング	haikingu
to hire	借ります	karimasu (dic. kariru*)
can I hire...?	…を借りられますか	...o kariraremasu ka?

hobby	趣味	shumi
holiday	休暇; ホリデー	kyuuka; horidee
on holiday	休暇中	kyuuka-chuu
national holiday	祭日	saijitsu
homesick	ホームシック	hoomushikku
honey	はちみつ	hachimitsu
honeymoon	ハネムーン; 新婚旅行	hanemuun; shinkon ryokoo
horse	馬	uma
horseradish (Japanese)	わさび	wasabi
hospital	病院	byooin
hostel	ユースホステル	yuusu hosuteru
hot	あつい	atsui
hotel	ホテル	hoteru
Japanese hotel (traditional)	旅館	ryokan
(B&B)	民宿	minshuku
hour	時間	jikan
one hour	一時間	ichi-jikan
two hours	二時間	ni-jikan
house	家	ie
house wine	ハウスワイン	hausu wain
how	どう; どうやって	doo; dooyatte
how much/many?	どのぐらいか	dono gurai?
how shall we get there?	どうやって行きましょうか	dooyatte ikimashoo ka?
hungry	おなかがすきます	onaka ga sukimasu (dic. onaka ga suku*)

I'm hungry	おなかがすいています	onaka ga suite imasu
hurry	急ぎます	isogimasu (dic. isogu*)
I'm in a hurry	急いでいます	isoide imasu
to hurt	痛みます	itamimasu (dic. itamu*)
my back hurts	背中が痛いです	senaka ga itai desu
husband (own)	主人	shujin
(somebody else's)	ご主人	go-shujin

I

I (informal)	わたし	watashi
(formal)	わたくし	watakushi
ice	氷; アイス	koori; aisu
ice cream	アイスクリーム	aisu kuriimu
identity card	身分証明書	mibun shoomei-sho
ill	病気	byooki
...is ill	…は病気です	...wa byooki desu
illegal	違法	ihoo
immediately	すぐに	sugu ni
important	大切 (な)	taisetsu (na)
imports	輸入	yunyuu
indigestion	消化不良	shooka furyoo
inflammation	炎症	enshoo
information	情報	joohoo
information office	案内所	annai-jo
injection	注射	chuusha

to be injured	怪我をします	kega o shimasu (dic. kega o suru*)
insect	昆虫	konchuu
insect repellent	虫除け	mushi-yoke
inside...	…の中に	...no naka ni
inside the car	車の中に	kuruma no naka ni
instant coffee	インスタントコーヒー	insutanto koohii
instructions (for use)	取扱説明書	toriatsukai setsumei-sho
insulin	インシュリン	inshurin
insurance	保険	hoken
insurance certificate	保険証	hokenshoo
international	国際的 (な)	kokusaiteki (na)
Internet	インターネット	intaanetto
Internet café	インターネットカフェ	intaanetto kafe
interpreter	通訳	tsuuyaku
interval (theatre)	休憩	kyuukei
to introduce (a person)	紹介します	shookai shimasu (dic. shookai suru*)
invitation	招待	shootai
to invite	招待します	shootai shimasu (dic. shootai suru*)
invoice	請求書	seikyuu-sho
Ireland	アイルランド	airurando
Irish (adj)	アイルランドの	airurando no
(person)	アイルランド人	airurando-jin

iron (for clothes)	アイロン	airon
(metal)	鉄	tetsu
ironmonger's	金物屋	kanamono-ya
island	島	shima
itemized bill	請求明細書	seikyuu meisaisho

J

jacket	ジャケット	jakketto
jam (food)	ジャム	jamu
traffic jam	交通渋滞	kootsuu juutai
January	一月	ichi-gatsu
Japan	日本	nihon; nippon
Japanese (language)	日本語	nihon-go
(adj)	日本の	nihon no
(person)	日本人	nihon-jin
jeweller's	宝石店	hooseki-ten
jewellery	宝石	hooseki
job	仕事	shigoto
to jog	ジョギングをします	jogingu o shimasu (dic. jogingu o suru*)
journey	旅行	ryokoo
juice (fruit)	ジュース	juusu
(of something)	汁; 液	shiru; eki
July	七月	shichi-gatsu
junction (roads)	交差点	koosaten
June	六月	roku-gatsu
just...	...だけ; ばかり	...dake; bakari

just two	二つだけ	futatsu dake
I've just arrived	ついたばかりです	tsuita bakari desu

K

key (for lock)	鍵	kagi
kilo	キロ	kiro
kilometre	キロメーター	kiromeetaa
kind (n)	種類	shurui
(adj)	親切 (な)	shinsetsu (na)
kitchen	台所	daidokoro
knickers	パンティー	pantii
knife	ナイフ	naifu
(Japanese)	包丁	hoochoo
knot	結び目; こぶ	musubi-me; kobu
to know (facts)		
do you know any good bars?	いいバーを知っていますか	ii baa o shitte imasu ka?
I don't know Tokyo	私は東京を知りません	watashi wa tookyoo o shirimasen
Korea	韓国	kankoku

L

label	ラベル	raberu
lace	レース	reesu
shoe lace	靴紐	kutsu-himo
ladies (toilet)	婦人用トイレ	fujin-yoo toire
lake	湖	mizuumi

land (n)	土地	tochi
language	言語; 言葉	gengo; kotoba
large	大きい	ookii
late	遅れます	okuremasu (dic. okureru*)
(time)	遅い	osoi
the train is late	電車が遅れています	densha ga okurete imasu
launderette	コインランドリー	koin randorii
laundry service	クリーニング	kuriiningu
lavatory	洗面所	semmenjo
lawyer	弁護士	bengoshi
leader (of group)	リーダー	riidaa
leaflet	チラシ	chirashi
leak (n) (of gas, liquid)	漏れ	more
to learn	学びます	manabimasu (dic. manabu*)
leather	革	kawa
to leave (depart)	出発します; 去ります	shuppatsu shimasu (dic. shuppatsu suru); sarimasu (dic. saru*)
(leave behind)	おいていきます	oite ikimasu (dic. oite iku*)
left	左	hidari
on/to the left	左に	hidari ni
left luggage (office)	手荷物一時預かり所	tenimotsu ichiji azukari-sho
leg	足	ashi

lens	レンズ	renzu
letter (mail)	手紙	tegami
letterbox	郵便受け	yuubin-uke
lettuce	レタス	retasu
library	図書館	toshokan
licence	免許証	menkyoshoo
to lie down	横になります	yoko ni narimasu (dic. yoko ni naru*)
life belt	救命ベルト	kyuumei-beruto
lifeboat	救命ボート	kyuumei-booto
lifeguard	ライフガード; 救助員	raifugaado; kyuujo-in
life jacket	ライフジャケット	raifu jakketo
lift (elevator)	エレベーター	erebeetaa
lighter	ライター	raitaa
do you have a lighter?	火 (ライター)がありますか	hi (raitaa) ga arimasu ka?
light bulb	電球	denkyuu
to like	好きです	suki desu
I like coffee	コーヒーが好きです	koohii ga suki desu
like this	このように; こういう風に	kono yoo ni; koo iu fuu ni
line (railway)	線	sen
(drawn)	ライン	rain
list	表; リスト	hyoo; risuto
to listen to...	…を聞きます	...o kikimasu (dic. kiku*)
litre	リットル	rittoru

L

a little	少し	sukoshi
to live (in a place)	住んでいます	sunde imasu (dic. sunde iru*)
I live in London	ロンドンに住んでいます	Rondon ni sunde imasu
to be alive	生きています	ikite imasu
he is alive	彼は生きています	kare wa ikite imasu
liver	レバー	rebaa
living room	居間	ima
lobster	ロブスター	robusutaa
local	地元	jimoto
lock (on door, box)	鍵; ロック	kagi; rokku
to lock	鍵をかけます	kagi o kakemasu (dic. kagi o kakeru*)
locker	ロッカー	rokkaa
long	長い	nagai
for a long time	長い間	nagai aida
to look for	探します	sagashimasu (dic. sagasu*)
loose (not fastened)	ゆるい	yurui
to lose	なくします	nakushimasu (dic. nakusu*)
I've lost...	…をなくしました	...o nakushimashita
lost (object)	なくした	nakushita
lost property office	紛失物取扱所	funshitsubutsu toriatsukai-sho
a lot	たくさん	takusan
lotion	ローション	rooshon
loud	うるさい	urusai

English - Japanese

love (n)	愛	ai
I love swimming	水泳が大好きです	suiei ga daisuki desu
luggage	荷物	nimotsu
luggage allowance	荷物制限	nimotsu seigen
luggage rack (in train)	網棚	amidana
lunch	昼ごはん; ランチ	hiru-gohan; ranchi
luxury	贅沢 (な)	zeitaku (na)

M

machine	機械	kikai
magazine	雑誌	zasshi
mail (n)	郵便	yuubin
by mail	郵便で	yuubin de
to make	作ります	tsukurimasu (dic. tsukuru*)
make-up	(お) 化粧	(o-)keshoo
man	人	hito
(male)	男の人	otoko no hito
manager	責任者; マネージャー	sekininsha; maneejaa
many	たくさんの	takusan no
map	地図	chizu
marathon	マラソン	marason
March	三月	san-gatsu
market	市場; マーケット	ichiba; maaketto
marmalade	マーマレード	maamareedo

M

to marry	結婚します	kekkon shimasu (dic. kekkon suru*)
to be married	結婚しています	kekkon shite imasu (dic. kekkon shite iru*)
martial arts	武道	budoo
mask	仮面; マスク	kamen; masuku
mass (in church)	ミサ	misa
match (game)	試合	shiai
matches	マッチ	matchi
to matter	気になります	ki ni narimasu (dic. ki ni naru*)
it doesn't matter	構いません	kamaimasen
mattress	マットレス	mattoresu
May	五月	go-gatsu
meal	食事	shokuji
to mean	意味します	imi shimasu (dic. imi suru*)
what does this mean?	これはどういう意味ですか	kore wa doo iu imi desu ka?
meat	(お) 肉	(o-)niku
mechanic	機械工; メカニック	kikaikoo; mekanikku
medical insurance	医療保険	iryoo-hoken
medicine	薬	kusuri
medieval	中世の	chuusei-no
to meet	会います	aimasu (dic. au*)
let's meet again	また会いましょう	mata aimashoo
meeting	ミーティング; 会議	miitingu; kaigi
member (of club, etc.)	会員; メンバー	kai-in; membaa

menu	メニュー	menyuu
message	伝言; メッセージ	dengon; messeeji
metre	メートル	meetoru
microwave	電子レンジ	denshi renji
midday	お昼	ohiru
at midday	お昼に	ohiru ni
middle-aged	中年の	chuunen no
midnight	真夜中	mayonaka
migraine	偏頭痛	henzutsuu
milk	ミルク; 牛乳	miruku; gyuunyuu
semi-skimmed	低脂肪牛乳	teishiboo gyuunyuu
soya milk	豆乳	toonyuu
millimetre	ミリメートル	mirimeetoru
million (n)	百万	hyaku-man
(adj)	百万の	hyaku-man-no
mineral water	ミネラルウォーター	mineraru wootaa
minibar	ミニバー	mini baa
minute	分	fun/pun
one minute	一分	ippun
two minutes	二分	nifun
mirror	鏡	kagami
to miss (train, etc.)	乗り遅れます	noriokuremasu (dic. noriokureru*)
missing (person)	行方不明	yukuefumei
mistake (n)	間違い	machigai
mobile phone	携帯電話	keitai denwa
modem	モデム	modemu

monastery	修道院	shuudooin
Monday	月曜日	getsu-yoobi
money	(お) 金	(o-)kane
I have no money	お金がありません	okane ga arimasen
month	月	tsuki
moon	月	tsuki
more	もっと	motto
more wine please	もっとワインをください	motto wain o kudasai
no more thank you	もう結構です	moo kekkoo desu
morning	朝	asa
in the morning	午前中に	gozenchuu ni
this morning	今朝	kesa
mosquito	蚊	ka
mother (own)	母	haha
(somebody else's)	お母さん	okaa-san
motorway	高速道路	koosoku dooro
mountain	山	yama
mountain bike	マウンテンバイク	maunten baiku
mouse (animal)	ねずみ	nezumi
(computer)	マウス	mausu
mouth	口	kuchi
Mr...	…氏; …さん	...-shi; ...-san
Mrs...	…さん; …夫人	...-san; ...-fujin
Ms...	…さん	...-san
much	多くの	ooku no
there's too much	多すぎます	oosugimasu

museum	博物館	hakubutsu-kan
mushroom	マッシュルーム	masshuruumu
(Japanese)	しいたけ	shiitake
music	音楽	ongaku
mussel	ムール貝	muuru-gai

N

nail (finger)	つめ	tsume
(metal)	釘	kugi
name	名前	namae
what's your name?	お名前は何ですか	o-namae wa nan desu ka?
nappy	オムツ	omutsu
narrow	狭い	semai
nationality	国籍	kokuseki
nausea	吐き気	hakike
near	近くに	chikaku ni
necessary	必要 (な)	hitsuyoo (na)
neck	首	kubi
necklace	ネックレス	nekkuresu
to need	必要です	hitsuyoo desu
I need...	…が必要です	...ga hitsuyoo desu
needle	針	hari
negative (photograph)	ネガ	nega
neighbour	近所	kinjo
nephew	甥	oi
never (adv)	絶対 …ません	zettai ... masen

I never drink wine	絶対ワインを飲みません	zettai wain o nomimasen
new	新しい	atarashii
news	ニュース; (お) 知らせ	nyuusu; (o-) shirase
newspaper	新聞	shimbun
New Year	新年	shinnen
New Zealand	ニュージーランド	nyuujiirando
New Zealander (person)	ニュージーランド人	nyuujiirando-jin
next	次	tsugi
next week	来週	raishuu
next year	来年	rainen
the next train	次の電車	tsugi no densha
night	夜	yoru
at night	夜に	yoru ni
last night	昨夜; 夕べ	sakuya; yuube
tomorrow night	明日の夜	ashita no yoru
nightclub	ナイトクラブ	naito kurabu
nightdress	寝巻き	nemaki
no	いいえ	iie
no, thank you	結構です	kekkoo desu
noisy	うるさい	urusai
non-alcoholic	アルコール抜き	arukooru nuki
non-smoking	禁煙	kin'en
non-smoking compartment	禁煙車両	kin'en sharyoo
noodles	麺	men

north	北	kita
Northern Ireland	北アイルランド	kita airurando
note (banknote)	紙幣	shihei
(letter)	メモ	memo
November	十一月	juuichi-gatsu
now	今	ima
nowadays	このごろ	konogoro
number (of)	数	kazu
number (1, 2, 3, etc.)	数字	suuji
nurse	看護師	kangoshi

O

object (thing)	物	mono
October	十月	juu-gatsu
octopus	たこ	tako
of (possessive)	…の	...no
off (light)	消えています	kiete imasu (dic. kiete iru*)
(food)	腐っています	kusatte imasu (dic. kusatte iru*)
office	オフィス; 事務所	ofisu; jimusho
often	よく	yoku
oil	油	abura
oil filter	オイルフィルター	oiru firutaa
OK	オーケー	ookei
I'm ok, it's ok	大丈夫です	daijoobu desu
ok, let's do that	オーケー、そうしましょう	ookei, soo shimashoo

O

English - Japanese

old (adj)	古い	furui
how old are you?	おいくつですか	oikutsu desu ka?
olive	オリーブ	oriibu
omelette	オムレツ	omuretsu
on (light)	ついています	tsuite imasu (dic. tsuite iru*)
on the table	テーブルの上に	teeburu no ue ni
one (adj)	ひとつの	hitotsu no
(n)	一	ichi
one-way ticket	片道切符	katamichi kippu
onion	たまねぎ	tamanegi
to open	開けます	akemasu (dic. akeru*)
the shop is open	営業中です	eigyoo-chuu desu
the door is open	ドアが開いています	doa ga aite imasu
operation (medical)	手術	shujutsu
opposite	反対	hantai
optician	メガネ屋	megane-ya
orange (colour)	オレンジ色	orenji-iro
(fruit)	オレンジ	orenji
orange juice	オレンジジュース	orenji juusu
out	外	soto
out of order	故障中	koshoo-chuu
he's out	彼は外出中です	kare wa gaishutsu-chuu desu
outdoor (pool, etc.)	野外	yagai
oven	オーブン	oobun
overnight train	夜行列車	yakoo ressha
oysters	牡蠣	kaki

P

Pacific Ocean	太平洋	taiheiyoo
packet	小包	kozutsumi
painful	痛い	itai
painkiller	鎮痛剤	chintsuuzai
painting	絵	e
(oil) **painting**	油絵	abura-e
palace	宮殿	kyuuden
pants (trousers)	ズボン	zubon
(men's underwear)	パンツ	pantsu
paper	紙	kami
paper handkerchief	ティッシュ	tisshu
paper towels	キッチンペーパー	kitchin peepaa
pardon?	すみません	sumimasen?
I beg your pardon!	すみません	sumimasen!
(didn't hear/ understand)	もう一度お願いします	moo ichido onegai shimasu
parents	両親	ryooshin
your parents	ご両親	go-ryooshin
park (garden)	公園	kooen
parking lot	駐車場	chuusha-joo
partner (wife, husband)	配偶者	haiguusha
party (evening)	パーティー	paatii
(group)	一行; 一団	ikkoo; ichidan
pass (permit)	許可証	kyokashoo
passenger	乗客	jookyaku

passport	パスポート	pasupooto
passport control	出入国管理所	shutsunyuukoku kanri-sho
path	小道	komichi
to pay	払います	haraimasu (dic. harau*)
payment	支払い	shiharai
payphone	公衆電話	kooshuu denwa
pear (Japanese)	梨	nashi
(western)	洋ナシ	yoonashi
pearl	真珠	shinju
pedestrian (n)	歩行者	hokoosha
pedestrian crossing	横断歩道	oodan-hodoo
pen	ペン	pen
pencil	鉛筆	empitsu
penicillin	ペニシリン	penishirin
pensioner	年金受給者	nenkin-jukyuu-sha
people	人々	hitobito
pepper (spice)	コショウ	koshoo
(vegetable)	ピーマン	piiman
per...	…につき	...ni tsuki
per hour	一時間につき	ichi-jikan ni tsuki
per person	一人につき	hitori ni tsuki
percent	パーセント	paasento
perfume	香水	koosui
period (menstruation)	生理	seiri
person	人	hito

personal organizer	電子手帳	denshi techoo
petrol	ガソリン	gasorin
petrol station	ガソリンスタンド	gasorin sutando
pharmacy	薬局	yakkyoku
phone (n)	電話	denwa
to phone	電話をかけます	denwa o kakemasu (dic. denwa o kakeru*)
phone box	電話ボックス	denwa bokkusu
phonecard	テレホンカード	terehon kaado
phone number	電話番号	denwa-bangoo
photocopy (n)	コピー	kopii
to photocopy	コピーをします	kopii o shimasu (dic. kopii o suru*)
photograph (n)	写真	shashin
to photograph	写真を撮ります	shashin o torimasu (dic. shashin o toru*)
pig	豚	buta
pillow	枕	makura
pineapple	パイナップル	painappuru
plan (of a building)	図面	zumen
to plan	企画します	kikaku shimasu (dic. kikaku suru*)
plane (aircraft)	飛行機	hikooki
plaster (sticking plaster)	バンドエイド	bando-eido
plastic bag	ポリ袋	pori-bukuro
platform (railway)	ホーム	hoomu
play (theatre)	劇	geki

plug (electrical)	プラグ; 差込	puragu; sashikomi
plug socket	コンセント	konsento
plum (Japanese, green)	梅	ume
(western, purple)	プラム	puramu
plumber	配管工; 水道屋	haikankoo; suidooya
pm (afternoon)	午後	gogo
poisonous	有毒（な）	yuudoku (na)
police	警察	keisatsu
police officer	警察官	keesatsu-kan
police station	警察署	keisatsu-sho
pool (swimming)	プール	puuru
pork	豚肉	buta-niku
portion (of food)	一人前	ichinin-mae
postcard	絵葉書	e-hagaki
post code	郵便番号	yuubin bangoo
post office	郵便局	yuubinkyoku
pound	ポンド	pondo
power cut	停電	teiden
power point	コンセント	konsento
prawn	海老	ebi
pregnant	妊娠している	ninshin shite iru
prescription	処方箋	shohoosen
present/gift	贈り物; プレゼント	okurimono; purezento
president (of a company)	社長	shachoo
pretty	かわいい	kawaii

price	値段	nedan
priest (Buddhist)	僧侶	sooryo
(Catholic)	神父	shimpu
(Protestant)	牧師	bokushi
prince	王子	ooji
princess	王女	oojo
private	個人の	kojin no
prize	賞品	shoohin
problem	問題	mondai
there's a problem	問題があります	mondai ga arimasu
programme (TV, etc.)	番組	bangumi
(computer)	プログラム	puroguramu
promise	約束	yakusoku
it's a promise	約束です	yakusoku desu
to pronounce	発音します	hatsuon shimasu (dic. hatsuon suru*)
how is it pronounced?	どのように発音しますか	dono yoo ni hatsuon shimasu ka?
Protestant	プロテスタント	purotesutanto
public holiday	祭日	saijitsu
public toilet	公衆トイレ	kooshuu toire
to pull	引きます	hikimasu (dic. hiku*)
puncture	パンク	panku
purse	財布	saifu
to push	押します	oshimasu (dic. osu*)
pushchair	バギー; ベビーカー	bagii; bebiikaa

Q

qualification	資格	shikaku
quality	品質	hinshitsu
queen	女王	jooo
question (n)	質問	shitsumon
queue	列	retsu
quickly	速く	hayaku
quiet (place)	静か（な）	shizuka (na)

R

rabies	狂犬病	kyookembyoo
race (sport)	競走	kyoosoo
(people)	人種	jinshu
radio	ラジオ	rajio
railway station	駅	eki
rain	雨	ame
it's raining	雨が降っています	ame ga futte imasu
rare (unique)	まれ	mare
(food)	レアー	reaa
rash (skin)	発疹	hasshin
raw	生	nama
razor	かみそり	kamisori
razor blades	かみそりのは	kamisori no ha
ready	準備できている	jumbi dekite iru
receipt	領収書; レシート	ryooshuusho; reshiito
reception (desk)	受付	uketsuke
receptionist	受付係	uketsuke-gakari

recipe	レシピ; 調理法	reshipi; choorihoo
to recommend	薦めます	susumemasu (dic. susumeru*)
what do you recommend?	何がお薦めですか	nani ga osusume desu ka?
record (music)	レコード	rekoodo
red (n)	赤	aka
(adj)	赤い	akai
reduction (for students, etc.)	割引	waribiki
refreshments	軽食	keishoku
refund	返金	henkin
I'd like a refund	返金してください	henkin shite kudasai
region	地域; 地方	chiiki; chihoo
to reimburse	返済します	hensai shimasu (dic. hensai suru*)
relative (family member)	親戚	shinseki
relatively (comparatively)	比較的	hikakuteki
reliable (person)	信頼できる	shinrai dekiru
religion	宗教	shuukyoo
to rent	借ります	karimasu (dic. kariru*)
rent (for house, flat)	家賃	yachin
to repair	修理します; 直します	shuuri shimasu (dic. shuuri suru*); naoshimasu (dic. naosu*)
to repeat	繰り返します	kurikaeshimasu (dic. kurikaesu*)

can you repeat that, please?	もう一度言ってください	moo ichido itte kudasai?
reservation	予約	yoyaku
reserved seat	指定席	shitei-seki
resort (seaside)	リゾート	rizooto
rest (relaxation)	休息	kyuusoku
to rest	休息します	kyuusoku shimasu (dic. kyuusoku suru*)
restaurant	レストラン	resutoran
restaurant car	食堂車	shokudoosha
retire	引退します	intai shimasu (dic. intai suru*)
to return (to go back)	帰ります; 戻ります	kaerimasu (dic. kaeru*); modorimasu (dic. modoru*)
(to give back)	返します	kaeshimasu (dic. kaesu*)
(to return a purchase)	返品します	hempin shimasu (dic. hempin suru*)
return ticket	往復切符	oofuku-kippu
reverse-charge call (collect call)	コレクトコール	korekuto kooru
rheumatism	リュウマチ	ryuumachi
rice	(お) 米	(o-)kome
(cooked)	ご飯	gohan
right (correct)	正しい	tadashii
on/to the right	右に	migi ni
ring (for finger)	指輪	yubiwa
river	川	kawa

road	道; 道路	michi; dooro
road sign	道路標識	dooro hyooshiki
to roast, bake or grill	焼きます	yakimasu (dic. yaku*)
room (in house, hotel)	部屋	heya
(space)	場所	basho
it takes up room	場所をとります	basho o torimasu
room service	ルームサービス	ruumu saabisu
rotten (meat, fruit)	腐った	kusatta
route	ルート; 順路	ruuto; junro
row (theatre, etc.)	列	retsu
royal	王室の	ooshitsu-no
rubbish	ごみ	gomi
(nonsense)	たわごと	tawagoto
rucksack	リュックサック	ryukkusakku
rush hour	ラッシュ	rasshu

S

safe (adj)	安全（な）	anzen (na)
safety belt	安全ベルト	anzen beruto
sailing (sport)	セーリング	seeringu
salad	サラダ	sarada
salary	サラリー; 給料	sararii; kyuuryoo
sale (in shops)	セール	seeru
salesman	セールスマン	seerusuman
(in store)	店員	ten-in

S

salmon	鮭	sake
salt	塩	shio
sandals	サンダル	sandaru
sandwich	サンドイッチ	sandoitchi
sanitary towel	生理用ナプキン	seiri-yoo napukin
sardine	イワシ	iwashi
satellite channels	衛星放送	eisei hoosoo
Saturday	土曜日	do-yoobi
sauce	ソース	soosu
to save (life)	救います	sukuimasu (dic. sukuu*)
(money)	蓄えます; 貯金します	takuwaemasu (dic. takuwaeru*); chokin shimasu (dic. chokin suru*)
to say	言います	iimasu (dic. iu*)
scales (for weighing)	はかり	hakari
scenery	景色	keshiki
school	学校	gakkoo
scissors	はさみ	hasami
Scotland	スコットランド	sukottorando
Scottish (adj)	スコットランドの	sukottorando no
screw (n)	ねじ	neji
screwdriver	ドライバー	doraibaa
scuba diving	スキューバダイビング	sukyuuba daibingu
sculpture (object)	彫刻	chookoku
sea	海	umi

seafood	シーフード; 海鮮料理	shiifuudo; kaisen-ryoori
seasickness	船酔い	funayoi
seaside	海辺	umibe
at the seaside	海辺で	umibe de
season (of year)	季節	kisetsu
season ticket	定期券	teiki-ken
seat	席	seki
seatbelt	シートベルト	shiitoberuto
seaweed	海草	kaisoo
secretary	秘書	hisho
security guard	警備員	keibi-in
to see	見ます	mimasu (dic. miru*)
self-catering	自炊	jisui
self-service	セルフサービス	serufu saabisu
to sell	売ります	urimasu (dic. uru*)
Sellotape®	セロテープ	seroteepu
to send	送ります	okurimasu (dic. okuru*)
to send someone off	見送ります	miokurimasu (dic. miokuru*)
senior citizen	高齢者	koorei-sha
September	九月	ku-gatsu
service (in restaurant, etc.)	サービス	saabisu
service charge	サービス料	saabisuryoo
set menu	定食	teishoku
sex (gender)	性別	seibetsu

shampoo	シャンプー	shampuu
to share	分担します; 分けます	buntan shimasu (dic. buntan suru*); wakemasu (dic. wakeru*)
shares (stocks)	株	kabu
to shave	そります	sorimasu (dic. soru*)
shaving cream	ヒゲそりクリーム	higesori kuriimu
sheet	シーツ	shiitsu
shellfish	魚介類	gyokairui
ship	船	fune
shirt	シャツ	shatsu
shoe	靴	kutsu
shoe polish	靴磨き	kutsu-migaki
shop	店	mise
shopping	買い物	kaimono
to go shopping	買い物します	kaimono shimasu (dic. kaimono suru*)
shopping trolley	ショッピングカート	shoppingu kaato
short cut	近道	chikamichi
shorts	半ズボン	hanzubon
shoulder	肩	kata
show (at theatre, etc.)	ショー	shoo
shower	シャワー	shawaa
shrimps	小エビ	ko-ebi
shrine	神社	jinja

to shut	閉めます	shimemasu (dic. shimeru*)
sick (ill)	病気	byooki
to be sick (vomit)	吐きます	hakimasu (dic. haku*)
sightseeing	観光	kankoo
signature	署名; サイン	shomei; sain
silk	絹	kinu
silver (n)	銀	gin
(adj)	銀の	gin no
single (person)	独身	dokushin
(bed, room)	一人用	hitori yoo
(ticket)	片道	katamichi
sink (bathroom, etc.)	流し; 洗面台	nagashi; semmendai
sister (own, younger)	妹	imooto
(own, older)	姉	ane
(somebody else's, younger)	妹さん	imooto-san
(somebody else's, older)	お姉さん	onee-san
sisters	姉妹	shimai
size	大きさ	ookisa
(clothes)	サイズ	saizu
to ski	スキーをします	sukii o shimasu (dic. sukii o suru*)
ski boots	スキー靴	sukii-gutsu
ski pass	リフト券	rifuto ken
skirt	スカート	sukaato
to sleep	寝ます	nemasu (dic. neru*)

sleeping bag	寝袋	nebukuro
sleeping pill	睡眠薬	suimin'yaku
slippers	スリッパ	surippa
slow	遅い	osoi
small	小さい	chiisai
smell (n)	におい	nioi
to smoke	タバコをすいます	tabako o suimasu (dic. tabako o suu*)
smoking	喫煙	kitsuen
no smoking	禁煙	kin'en
snack	軽食	keishoku
snow (n)	雪	yuki
it's snowing	雪が降っています	yuki ga futte imasu
soap	石鹸	sekken
soap powder	粉石鹸	kona sekken
sober (not drunk)	素面	shirafu
sock	靴下	kutsushita
soda water	炭酸水	tansansui
soft drink	ソフトドリンク	sofuto dorinku
something	何か	nanika
sometimes	時々	tokidoki
son (own)	息子	musuko
(somebody else's)	息子さん	musuko-san
song	歌	uta
soon	すぐ	sugu
sore head	頭痛	zutsuu
sore throat	のどの痛み	nodo no itami

sorry	すみません	sumimasen
I'm sorry	すみません	sumimasen
soup	スープ	suupu
south	南	minami
South Africa	南アフリカ	minami afurika
South African (person)	南アフリカ人	minami afurika-jin
souvenir	お土産; 記念品	o-miyage; kinen-hin
soy sauce	醤油	shooyu
spanner	レンチ	renchi
to speak	話します	hanashimasu (dic. hanasu*)
do you speak English?	英語を話せますか	eigo o hanasemasu ka?
speciality	専門	semmon
speed limit	制限速度	seigen sokudo
to spell	綴ります	tsuzurimasu (dic. tsuzuru*)
how is it spelt?	綴りを教えてください	tsuzuri o oshiete kudasai?
to spend (money)	(お金を) 使います	(okane o) tsukaimasu (dic. tsukau*)
spicy	辛い	karai
spirits (alcohol)	蒸留酒	jooryuushu
spoon	スプーン	supuun
sport	スポーツ	supootsu
sprain (ankle, etc.)	捻挫	nenza
spring (season)	春	haru

hot spring (water)	温泉	onsen
squash (game, drink)	スカッシュ	sukasshu
squid	イカ	ika
stadium	スタジアム; 競技場	sutajiamu; kyoogijoo
stamps (for letters)	切手	kitte
star (in sky)	星	hoshi
(film)	スター	sutaa
station	駅	eki
stationer's	文房具屋	bumboogu-ya
statue	像	zoo
steak	ステーキ	suteeki
steep	険しい	kewashii
stereo	ステレオ	sutereo
sting (n)	刺し傷	sashi-kizu
stomach	おなか	onaka
stomach ache	腹痛	fukutsuu
storm	嵐	arashi
straight on	まっすぐ	massugu
strange (odd)	変（な）	hen (na)
strawberry	イチゴ	ichigo
street	通り	toori
string (for wrapping)	紐	himo
strong (person)	強い	tsuyoi
(material)	丈夫（な）	joobu (na)
stuck (jammed)	詰まっている	tsumatte iru
student	学生	gakusei
suburbs	郊外	koogai

subway (metro)	地下鉄	chikatetsu
suddenly	突然	totsuzen
sugar	砂糖	satoo
sugar-free	無糖	mutoo
suit	スーツ	suutsu
suitcase	スーツケース	suutsukeesu
summer	夏	natsu
sun	太陽	taiyoo
to sunbathe	日光浴をします	nikkooyoku o shimasu (dic. nikkooyoku o suru*)
suntan	日焼け	hiyake
Sunday	日曜日	nichi-yoobi
sunglasses	サングラス	sangurasu
sunscreen	日焼け止め	hiyake-dome
sunstroke	日射病	nisshabyoo
supermarket	スーパー	suupaa
supper (dinner)	夕食	yuushoku
surgery (of doctor)	診察室	shinsatsu-shitsu
surname	苗字	myooji
sweet (not savoury)	甘い	amai
sweetener	甘味料	kammiryoo
sweets	お菓子	o-kashi
to swim	泳ぎます	oyogimasu (dic. oyogu*)
swimsuit	水着	mizugi
to switch off	切ります	kirimasu (dic. kiru*)
to switch on	入れます	iremasu (dic. ireru*)
synagogue	ユダヤ教会堂	yudaya-kyookaidoo

T

table	テーブル	teeburu
to take (time)	かかります	kakarimasu (dic. kakaru*)
(photos)	撮ります	torimasu (dic. toru*)
how long does it take?	どのぐらいかかりますか	dono gurai kakarimasu ka?
to talk	話します	hanashimasu (dic. hanasu*)
tampon	タンポン	tampon
tangerine	みかん	mikan
tap	蛇口	jaguchi
tape (sticky)	粘着テープ	nenchaku teepu
to taste (of something)	味わいます	ajiwaimasu (dic. ajiwau*)
to taste (something)	食べてみます	tabete mimasu (dic. tabete miru*)
tax	税金	zeikin
tax-free	免税	menzei
taxi	タクシー	takushii
by taxi	タクシーで	takushii de
taxi driver	タクシーの運転手	takushii no untenshu
taxi rank	タクシー乗り場	takushii noriba
tea (green)	お茶	o-cha
(English)	紅茶	koocha
teacher	先生	sensei
teeth	歯	ha
telephone (n)	電話	denwa

English	Japanese	Romanization
telephone box	電話ボックス	denwa bokkusu
telephone directory	電話帳	denwa choo
telephone number	電話番号	denwa bangoo
television	テレビ	terebi
to tell	言います	iimasu (dic. iu*)
temperature (fever)	熱	netsu
I have a temperature	熱があります	netsu ga arimasu
temple	(お) 寺	(o-)tera
tennis	テニス	tenisu
tennis court	テニスコート	tenisu kooto
tennis racket	テニスラケット	tenisu raketto
tent	テント	tento
terminal (airport)	ターミナル	taaminaru
thank you	ありがとう	arigatoo
thank you very much	(どうも) ありがとうございます	(doomo) arigatoo gozaimasu
that one (object near the listener)	それ	sore
(away from the listener and speaker)	あれ	are
theatre	劇場	gekijoo
thermometer	温度計	ondokei
thick (paper, board)	厚い	atsui
(rope, cord)	太い	futoi
(sauce)	濃い	koi
thief	泥棒	doroboo

English	Japanese	Romaji
thin (paper, sauce)	薄い	usui
(rope, cord)	細い	hosoi
thing	物	mono
my things	私のもの	watashi no mono
thirsty	のどが渇きます	nodo ga kawakimasu (dic. nodo ga kawaku*)
I'm thirsty	のどが渇きました	nodo ga kawakimashita
this one	これ	kore
throat	のど	nodo
thunder	雷	kaminari
thunderstorm	雷雨	raiu
Thursday	木曜日	moku-yoobi
ticket	切符; チケット	kippu; chiketto
ticket office	切符売り場	kippu uriba
ticket vending machine	券売機	kembai-ki
tight	きつい	kitsui
tights	タイツ	taitsu
time	時間	jikan
this time	今回	konkai
what time is it?	何時ですか	nan-ji desu ka?
timetable	スケジュール	sukejuuru
(train, etc.)	時刻表	jikoku-hyoo
tinned	缶詰	kanzume
tinfoil	アルミホイル	arumi hoiru
tin-opener	缶きり	kankiri
tired	疲れます	tsukaremasu (dic. tsukareru*)

I'm tired	疲れました	tsukaremashita
tissue	ティッシュ	tisshu
toast (bread)	トースト	toosuto
tobacconist's	タバコ屋	tabako-ya
today	今日	kyoo
toilet (informal)	トイレ	toire
(polite)	お手洗い	o-tearai
toilet paper	トイレットペーパー	toiretto peepaa
toiletries	化粧品	keshoohin
toll (motorway)	通行料	tsuukooryoo
tomato	トマト	tomato
tomorrow	明日	ashita
tomorrow afternoon	明日の午後	ashita no gogo
tomorrow morning	明日の朝	ashita no asa
tomorrow night	明日の夜	ashita no yoru
tonight	今夜; 今晩	kon'ya; komban
tooth	歯	ha
toothache	歯痛	haita
toothbrush	歯ブラシ	haburashi
toothpaste	歯磨き粉	hamigakiko
torch	懐中電灯	kaichuu-dentoo
tough (meat)	かたい	katai
tour (sightseeing)	ツアー	tsuaa
tourist	観光客	kankoo-kyaku
tourist office	観光案内所	kankoo-annai-sho
towel	タオル	taoru

town	町	machi
town centre	町の中心	machi no chuushin
town plan	町の地図	machi no chizu
toy	おもちゃ	omocha
tracksuit	トレーニングウェアー	toreeningu ueaa
tradition	伝統	dentoo
traffic	交通	kootsuu
traffic jam	交通渋滞	kootsuu-juutai
traffic lights	信号	shingoo
train	電車	densha
translation	翻訳	hon'yaku
translator	翻訳家	hon'yaku-ka
to travel	旅行します	ryokoo shimasu (dic. ryokoo suru*)
travel agent's	旅行代理店	ryokoo dairiten
traveller's cheque	トラベラーズチェック	toraberaazu chekku
tree	木	ki
trip	旅行	ryokoo
trousers	ズボン	zubon
trout	ます	masu
true (real)	本当	hontoo
Tuesday	火曜日	ka-yoobi
tuna	マグロ	maguro
to turn off (light, etc.)	消します	keshimasu (dic. kesu*)

to turn on (light, etc.)	つけます	tsukemasu (dic. tsukeru*)
tweezers	毛抜き	kenuki
twin-bed room	ツインベッドの部屋	tsuin beddo no heya
tyre	タイヤ	taiya

U

ulcer	潰瘍	kaiyoo
umbrella	傘	kasa
uncle (own)	おじ	oji
(somebody else's)	おじさん	oji-san
underground (metro)	地下鉄	chikatetsu
to understand	わかります	wakarimasu (dic. wakaru*)
I don't understand	わかりません	wakarimasen
do you understand?	わかりますか	wakarimasu ka?
underwear	下着	shitagi
unemployed	無職	mushoku
United Kingdom	英国; イギリス	eikoku; igirisu
United States of America	アメリカ; 合衆国	amerika; gasshuukoku
university	大学	daigaku
to unpack (case)	荷物を開けます	nimotsu o akemasu (dic. nimotsu o akeru*)
urgent	緊急	kinkyuu

V

vacancy (in hotel)	空き室	akishitsu
vaccination	予防注射	yoboo-chuusha
valid (passport, etc.)	有効（な）	yuukoo (na)
valuables	貴重品	kichoo-hin
van	バン; ワゴン車	ban; wagon-sha
vase	花瓶	kabin
vegetable	野菜	yasai
vegetarian	ベジタリアン; 菜食主義者	bejitarian; saishoku-shugi-sha
vehicle	乗り物	norimono
very	大変; とても	taihen; totemo
video	ビデオ	bideo
video game	ビデオゲーム	bideo geemu
village	村	mura
vinegar	酢	su
virus	ウイルス	uirusu
visa	ビザ	biza
to visit	たずねます	tazunemasu (dic. tazuneru*)
visitor	客	kyaku
(tourist)	観光客	kankoo-kyaku
vitamin	ビタミン	bitamin

W

wage	賃金; 給料	chingin; kyuuryo
waist	ウエスト	uesuto

waiter	ウエイター	ueitaa
to wait for...	...を待ちます	...o machimasu (dic. matsu*)
waiting room	待合室	machiai-shitsu
waitress	ウエイトレス	ueitoresu
to wake up	起きます	okimasu (dic. okiru*)
Wales	ウェールズ	weeruzu
to walk	歩きます	arukimasu (dic. aruku*)
to go for a walk	散歩します	sampo shimasu (dic. sampo suru*)
wallet	財布	saifu
to want	欲しいです	hoshii desu
wardrobe	洋服ダンス	yoofuku-dansu
warm	暖かい	atatakai
to wash	洗います	araimasu (dic. arau*)
washing machine	洗濯機	sentaku-ki
washing powder	粉石けん	kona-sekken
washing-up liquid	液体洗剤	ekitai-senzai
wasp	スズメバチ	suzumebachi
watch (on wrist)	腕時計	udedokei
to watch TV	テレビを見ます	terebi o mimasu (dic. miru*)
water	水	mizu
hot water	お湯	oyu
water heater	湯沸かし器	yuwakashiki
watermelon	すいか	suika
waterproof	防水	boosui
water-skiing	水上スキー	suijoo-sukii

W

English - Japanese

way (manner)	仕方	shikata
(route)	方向	hookoo
way in	入口	iriguchi
way out	出口	deguchi
we	私たち	watashi-tachi
weak (physically)	弱い	yowai
(tea, etc.)	うすい	usui
weather	天気	tenki
weather forecast	天気予報	tenki yohoo
website	ウェブサイト	webusaito
wedding	結婚式	kekkon-shiki
Wednesday	水曜日	sui-yoobi
week	週	shuu
weekday	平日	heijitsu
weekend	週末	shuumatsu
weekly	毎週	maishuu
weight	重さ	omosa
well	よい	yoi
well done!	よくできました	yoku dekimashita!
I am well	元気です	genki desu
Welsh (person)	ウェールズ人	weeruzu-jin
west (n)	西	nishi
wet	ぬれた	nureta
what	何	nani; nan
what is it?	それは何ですか	sore wa nan desu ka?
wheel (of car)	車輪	sharin
wheelchair	車椅子	kuruma isu

when	いつ	itsu
where	どこ	doko
which one (of two)	どちら	dochira
(of three or more)	どれ	dore
which is it?	どれですか	dore desu ka?
whisky	ウイスキー	uisukii
white (n)	白	shiro
(adj)	白い	shiroi
who	誰	dare
whose	誰の	dare no
whose is it?	誰のですか	dare no desu ka?
why	なぜ; どうして	naze; dooshite
wide	広い	hiroi
widow	未亡人	miboojin
wife (own)	妻	tsuma
(somebody else's)	奥さん	oku-san
to win	勝ちます	kachimasu (dic. katsu*)
wind (air)	風	kaze
window	窓	mado
windscreen	フロントガラス	furonto garasu
windscreen wipers	ワイパー	waipaa
windsurfing	ウィンドサーフィン	uindo saafin
wine	ワイン	wain
red wine	赤ワイン	aka wain
white wine	白ワイン	shiro wain
wine list	ワインリスト	wain risuto

winter	冬	fuyu
with... (a person)	…と一緒に	...to issho ni
woman	女の人	onna no hito
wonderful	すばらしい	subarashii
wood	木	ki
wool	毛; ウール	ke; uuru
word	単語	tango
to work (person)	働きます	hatarakimasu (dic. hataraku*)
(machine, car)	動きます	ugokimasu (dic. ugoku*)
world	世界	sekai
wrist	手首	tekubi
to write	書きます	kakimasu (dic. kaku*)
writer (author)	著者	chosha
wrong	悪い	warui

X

x-ray	レントゲン	rentogen

Y

year	年	nen; toshi
for one year	一年間	ichi-nen-kan
one year old	一歳	issai
five years old	五歳	go-sai
this year	今年	kotoshi
next year	来年	rainen

last year	去年	kyonen
yellow (n)	黄色	kiiro
(adj)	黄色い	kiiroi
yes	はい	hai
yes, please	はい、お願いします	hai, onegai shimasu
yesterday	昨日	kinoo
yet	まだ	mada
not yet	まだです	mada desu
youth hostel	ユースホステル	yuusu hosuteru

Z

zebra crossing	横断歩道	oodan hodoo
zero	ゼロ; 零	zero; rei
zip	チャック; ファスナー	chakku; fasunaa
zone	ゾーン; 地帯	zoon; chitai
zoo	動物園	doobutsu-en

Language learning on the go

Ideal for beginners | from £14.99
collins.co.uk/languagelearning

Collins